CPHQ Study Guide
2022-2023

Updated Review + 420 Test Questions and Detailed Answer Explanations for the Certified Professional in Healthcare Quality Exam (Includes 3 Full-Length Practice Exams)

Table of Contents

Chapter 1: Introduction

Those who hold Certified Professional in Healthcare Quality (CPHQ) certification are identified as professionals who understand health-care quality, practices and principles.

How Do You Get CPHQ Certification?

To become a CPHQ-certified professional, you must take a CPHQ certification exam. There are no eligibility requirements for candidates, but it is recommended that you have at least two years of experience in the field of health-care quality. This exam is conducted by the Healthcare Quality Certification Board (HQCB).

How long does it take to get CPHQ certification?

It takes three hours to complete the CPHQ exam. It consists of 140 multiple-choice questions (MCQs), out of which 15 are pretest questions, which are not added to your final score.

How much does the CPHQ exam cost?

NAHQ members pay $423. Nonmembers pay $529. An additional $25 fee is required if you apply through mail. There is no additional fee for online applicants.

How to sign up for the CPHQ exam

Visit the NAHQ website to sign up for the CPHQ exam online.

What is the pass rate for the CPHQ exam?

The passing rate of the CPHQ exam is 62 percent. Many candidates attempt the exam more than once until they pass.

What is a passing score for the CPHQ exam?

The score required to pass the exam varies from year to year. It mostly depends upon the exam's difficulty level. On average, you are required to answer 73 percent of questions correctly to pass the certification exam.

Can You Reattempt the CPHQ Exam?

If you fail on your first try, you can reattempt the CPHQ exam after three months. To retake this test, you need to submit a new application along with the full exam fee.

The Contents of this CPHQ Guide

To pass this challenging test, thorough preparation is necessary. *CPHQ Study Guide 2020 and 2021 - CPHQ Study Guide* is divided into different chapters, each of which covers a topic you will be tested on. The guide also includes practice questions.

Our guide includes everything you need to pass your CPHQ exam. It covers critical information required to pass the exam, including principles, concepts and procedures. It also covers vocabulary you are expected to master before taking the exam.

Detailed chapters with specific information

This CPHQ guide covers all the specific information you need to pass your exam. Every concept is explained in detail. Chapters are laid out in a logical fashion to create a flow, as one chapter precedes the next. This book is written with accessibility and technical accuracy in mind. The language is simple and easy to understand.

Practice test questions with explanations

This test guide also includes practice questions that help you assess your knowledge. Each of these questions was developed with past tests in mind. Every answer is thoroughly explained so that you can understand the logic behind a given principle. These questions prepare you for the questions you are expected to answer on the actual exam. Every answer is explained in detail.

CPHQ Study Guide 2020 and 2021 - CPHQ Study Guide is an excellent investment if you want to be successful on your CPHQ exam.

Chapter 2: Importance of Quality in Health Care

What Is Health Care?

Health care is defined as an organized process of providing medical care to people and communities. A health care career includes much more than just doctors, frontline clinicians and nurses. Paramedics, chiropractors, therapists, administrators and technical professionals all work together to help people live healthy lives.

All health-care professions require formal education. Professionals, such as surgeons, ophthalmologists, and anesthesiologists, need over 12 years of higher education. But various other professions require only a few months of preparation. To enter fields like EKG and cardio-phlebotomy, special tech certifications are required. These certifications take 10 to 12 weeks to earn.

The Role of Nurses in Health Care

Nursing has been around for over two centuries as a career, but the role of nurses has greatly evolved over that time. Centuries ago, nurses worked in convents; they were associated with hospitals run by a church. Figures like Florence Nightingale lobbied to provide nurses with proper training. She believed, to improve the overall health-care sector, it was essential to provide better working conditions and training to those who opted for nursing as a profession.

Today, the role of nurses and the way they are educated has entirely changed. Bachelor of Science (BSN) in Nursing and Associate Degree in Nursing (ADN) programs have replaced hospitals' diploma programs. Various advanced nursing professions have also been introduced, including nurse anesthetist and nurse practitioners. These professions require a master's and, in some cases, even a doctorate degree.

Nursing in Modern Health Care

Today, nurses have far greater responsibility and autonomy than they had in the past. They share a more collaborative relationship with physicians, surgeons and other health-care workers than they used to and serve as a vital link between the patient and the doctor.

Responsibilities of a Nurse

Listed below are some of the responsibilities assigned to a nurse.

Nurses educate patients

Nurses are the first person you see when you visit a doctor. A skilled nurse knows how to talk to patients and get to know them. This helps the doctor uncover important health information. Once the doctor checks patients, it is the nurse's responsibility to educate patients on how they need to take medication. Nurses make sure that patients understand their health condition and treatment so that patients can then help care for themselves.

Nurses serve as frontline health-care workers—they are the first to notice a change in a patient's health condition and are also the first to take any action when a patient is in critical condition.

Patient advocacy

Out of all health-care workers, nurses spend the most time with patients. This provides them with insights into patients' concerns, wants, needs and behaviors. Patient advocacy is a pillar of nursing.

A nurse provides advocacy in various forms, including having a conversation with patients and their families, uncovering important details during this conversation and relaying the acquired information to the doctor.

If a medication does not work how it is supposed to, nurses contact pharmacists to talk it through. Patient advocacy also means helping patients find other health-care providers as necessary. Nurses also ensure that patients have given their consent to start treatment before it begins.

Low health literacy, the inability to understand basic health-related information and make informed decisions, is one of the biggest challenges health-care workers face every day. It hinders patients' ability to understand the information required for a quick recovery. Sometimes patients feel intimidated and cannot ask the right questions. Nurses are responsible for helping patients feel comfortable with the parameters of both their conditions and treatments.

Monitoring patient health

Monitoring a patient's health is one of the most crucial nursing responsibilities. Nurses stay with patients throughout their illness and monitor their health. They keep track of patients' conditions day in and day out, whereas physicians check patients only from time to time.

Nurses' responsibilities include everything from charting patients' vital signs to making sure individuals are taking their medication.

The assessments made by nurses are summarized and added to patients' permanent medical records. Nurses are responsible for consistently updating records and communicating patient information to the overall health-care team.

More autonomy

Today nurses have a greater degree of autonomy than ever. They are the first ones to uncover any problem patients are dealing with during a hospital stay. Nurses are the first ones to act immediately when it comes to stabilizing patients.

In certain cases, nurses are allowed to act without seeking permission from the doctor. For example, they can administer magnesium to patients with dangerously low magnesium levels without a doctor's approval.

Repercussions of Not Maintaining Quality in Health Care

Most health-care professionals still rely on pen, paper and their memory to issue reports, orders and treatment plans. Integrating the right technology can redesign an improved health-care system with reliable, cost-effective and maintainable solutions.

Listed below are some of the repercussions associated with poor-quality health care.

Misdiagnosis

Poor quality health-care services result in incorrect or delayed diagnoses. Most of these errors have the potential to put a patient's life at risk. For example, a misdiagnosis can result in a loss of opportunity to treat cancer at an early stage. In severe cases, misdiagnosis also leads to extended hospitalization and even death. The likelihood of a misdiagnosis can be reduced by maintaining the quality of health care.

Dissatisfied patients

This consequence arises when staff fail to meet patients' needs. This happens when health-care professionals fail to listen closely to what their patients are saying. This lack of communication happens because of a variety of reasons, such as:

- Ineffective policies

- Language barriers

- Workload pressure

- Conflicts between staff members

- Poor documentation

- Poor communication systems within hospitals.

<u>Negative reputation</u>

Maintaining a good reputation is a priority for every health-care organization. With easy access to the internet, patients can write a negative review if they do not find services satisfactory. These reviews can damage the reputation of a health-care business.

According to research, over 82 percent of adults read online reviews on social media before trying a health-care provider. Research has also revealed that social media reviews influence 88 percent of potential patients when they are choosing a health-care provider. These patients book an appointment only when they read positive reviews.

What Is Quality Improvement in Health Care?

To bring quality improvement to the health-care system, we have to improve the following aspects:

- Safety

- Effectiveness

- Efficiency.

Specialized tools and methods are required to help improve health-care systems. Electronic medical record software integration is a user-centric approach. It can secure patients' health-care data and help them keep track of vital information.

How Quality Improvement in Health Care Helps

Quality improvement in health care is a planned approach used by a health-care institution to improve, assess and monitor quality health-care service delivery. It is a continuous process that includes a series of steps that enhance a health-care system's performance level.

By continuously upgrading health-care services, an organization can produce better-quality results. The utilization of technology and advanced tools is essential to eradicate ineffective and outdated concepts formerly used in the health-care sector.

Chapter 3: Ways to Support Organizational Commitment to Quality

The Responsibilities of Health-Care Organizations in Maintaining Quality

A health-care organization's success depends upon its members—the people who work together as a team. Each team member is assigned a responsibility in achieving the highest patient-care standards. To make that happen, the administration needs to implement solid quality control measures for both the health-care service providers and the equipment.

Every health-care organization has different administrative needs. However, across all these organizations, the basic framework and principles are the same. A health-care organization's goal should be to create a workplace where both staff and patients feel safe.

Let's discuss the responsibilities of a health-care organization when it comes to maintaining quality.

Health-Care Organization Responsibilities for Maintaining Quality

A health-care organization's most important duties are listed below.

Introduction of Concrete Processes in the System

The health-care profession requires sensitivity and compassion, so common sense and employee intuition are of the utmost importance. Implementation of strict rules can make health-care professionals feel trapped. This can result in a loss of sensitivity toward patients.

Well-planned quality control processes protect both patients and caregivers. They allow health-care workers to provide patient care to the best of their abilities. These processes are designed to define individual roles, responsibilities and activities within the health-care setting.

For example, the implementation of quality control measures ensures that equipment and rooms are sterilized when a patient is discharged. Technicians and doctors double-check test results to prevent the transfer of disease.

The creation of these processes depends upon the health-care settings. Keeping these settings in mind, protocols for quality control are established. These protocols are based on the health-care policies followed by your city or state. The ultimate goal of these processes is to achieve excellence in providing the highest-quality patient care.

Maintaining a clean work atmosphere

Maintaining a clean work environment goes beyond sterilizing equipment and surgical rooms every few hours. A health-care organization's responsibility is to encourage workers to play their part in keeping every area hazard-free.

To create and maintain a clean workplace environment, a health-care organization needs to do much more than just try to meet minimal standards. It needs to encourage a work culture that promotes a clean environment for both workers and patients. The staff needs to be educated to improve their morale and professionalism. Special training should be given to staff to teach them to prevent spills, pick up equipment and avoid tripping hazards. The safety program established to reduce clutter should include procedures for spill clean-ups and hazard removal.

Performing unplanned equipment tests

One of the biggest hazards patients are exposed to in a health-care facility is access to equipment. Without proper supervision, equipment is often incorrectly used, which compromises patient safety. Health-care organizations can ensure compliance by holding impromptu equipment tests. Health-care workers will be more careful in equipment and technology usage when their expertise is spontaneously spot-checked once in a while. Employees should be notified if they make an error, and they should be allowed to correct their mistakes.

Keeping track of the inventory of equipment spare parts

Quality control programs should always include an inventory of the equipment an organization requires to provide on-time, optimal health-care services.

The organization needs to hire employees who know how to replace spare parts. Staff should know where the equipment spare parts can be found. If specialized professionals are required to replace the parts, staff should know whom to contact in case of an equipment breakdown. Alternative protocols should be available when equipment is being fixed.

Training the managers

Quality control measures are useless if they are not appropriately implemented. A health-care organization's management team is responsible for designing and implementing these processes. To ensure these processes are correctly implemented, it is crucial to ensure perfection at every stage of the quality assurance process. This makes it essential to train and support managers who can effectively implement these processes.

The organization needs to introduce proper management training systems to streamline the process of running a health-care institution. Managers should be trained to hire the right talent and help any employee who is struggling. The goal should be to provide high-quality patient care.

Participation in Organization-Wide Strategic Planning

The size, complexity and level of the organization define the strategic planning processes to be implemented. Each unit of a complex health-care organization will require its own strategic plan. It is the responsibility of the unit leader to design and apply the process.

The strategic planning process introduced in an organization has to be programmable, all-inclusive, organized and rational. It should be designed to achieve short-, medium- and long-term goals. The ultimate goal of the strategic planning process should be to transform the health-care organization of the future.

How to Begin with Strategic Planning

There are various aspects that a health-care unit leader must consider when starting strategic planning. Creating an effective and long-lasting strategic plan requires a thorough understanding of a plan's conceptual aspects. Without this understanding, the leader will implement a plan in a superficial manner, which is one of the biggest reasons why strategic plans fail. Listed below are the aspects that should be considered before designing and implementing a strategic plan.

Overcoming challenges

Strategic processes are put in place to streamline operations within a health-care organization. One individual cannot manage these organization-wide plans. For the plan to be effective, each unit of the organization requires a leader who can supervise the process and ensure a smooth, functioning unit. Each unit must work together to create an environment that promotes productivity and adequate health care.

Achieving a clear transformational goal

Defining the purpose of a strategic plan is also very important. The purpose of a strategic plan should be purely transformational and include:

- Identification of current characteristics based on the organizational settings

- Identification of the vision the organization wishes to achieve in the future

- A defined road map and the actions to be taken to achieve the desired vision.

Reasons to Use Strategic Planning

There are five reasons why a health-care organization requires strategic planning.

To satisfy patients

Patients have many options to choose from. Access to vast amounts of information is creating more demanding clients. Organizations need to be prepared to treat educated patients who have the power to choose their health-care providers. By implementing an effective strategic planning process, these organizations can keep pace with the growing demands of more informed patients.

To compete with skilled competitors

The health-care industry is more competitive than ever before. Health-care organizations need strategic plans to access health-care professionals with market-leading skills and knowledge. They also need to stay current with the latest technologies used by their market competitors. By creating a strategic plan, health-care organizations can keep up in a highly competitive health-care environment.

To allocate limited resources

A strategic plan is required to allocate resources rationally to operate as an efficient health-care organization.

To ensure the best patient experience

With patients becoming more aware and informed as time passes, health-care organizations' focus has shifted from the quality of products and services to the satisfaction of the client. Patients' experience matters more than ever today.

To create a plan that complements the organization's size and complexity

With increasing health-care demands, health-care organizations are getting bigger. This has made these organizations even more complex. A strategic plan is required to divide a large production unit into highly functional subunits. These units' leaders should be trained to collaborate to deliver the highest-quality primary care for various health issues.

Another source of complexity arises from collaborating with primary care for a range of diseases, especially chronic ones.

The process of strategic planning can be divided into the following steps.

1. Formulation of strategy
2. Analysis of the external environment
3. Analysis of the internal environment
4. SWOT analysis
5. Deciding strategic alternatives
6. Defining strategic areas and objectives.

Alignment of Quality and Safety Activities

Aligning quality and safety activities is the only way for a health-care organization to create a culture where patients feel safe. There are a few practices that align quality improvement practices with safety activities:

- Simplifying and standardizing process, supplies and equipment within a health-care organization

- Implementing policies that impel health-care professionals to work ethically

- Integrating the right technology to reduce memory reliance and other cognitive aspects

- Ensuring effective communication between health-care stakeholders to promote awareness regarding patient safety

- Training and equipping medical professionals to improve their performance

- Holding interdisciplinary programs to encourage effective collaboration between subunits

- Allowing managers and leaders to contribute to the process of quality improvement

- Maintaining the right balance between fairness and accountability within an organizational culture

- Promoting effective collection, monitoring and error evaluation of patient safety data

- Introducing methods that reduce errors.

Engagement of Stakeholders for Ensuring the Highest Quality Health-Care Delivery

Stakeholders in health and social care include:

1. Government

Government institutions are the biggest stakeholders in the health-care sector. Creating an effective health-care system on a state level requires support from policymakers. However, it is the health-care organization's responsibility to communicate to the government the issues faced while providing health care to patients.

By engaging the government, these institutions ensure that their activities and strategic plans match national priorities. Organizations need to be familiar with the coordination mechanisms that exist within states and localities.

2. The service delivery system

The service delivery system is an important stakeholder in health care. It includes several individuals involved in establishing an effective emergency communication response (for example, service providers and managers).

Service providers include everyone from frontline health workers to paid staff and volunteers. They support and treat those affected by an emergency. The service delivery system serves as an effective tool in educating and helping communities to take the right protective measures.

Health facilities operate at a variety of levels, including national, local and subnational. Each of the facilities provides a variety of services, including state-level, faith-based and private services. Health-care organizations should communicate with these facilities at their level of operation. This communication will result in synchronizing messages, practices and procedures that lay the foundation of a uniform health-care system across the nation.

3. United Nations agencies

Various agencies work under the United Nations. They collaborate with government institutions to increase the capacity and potential of their health-care systems. These agencies support the government and suggest health-care policies that ensure effective communication, social mobilization, harmonization of activities and duplication prevention.

Bilateral organizations also play a significant role in strengthening the government's capacity for providing effective health-care services. They promote emergency preparedness and effective communication.

4. Nongovernmental organizations

Nongovernmental (NGO) and local organizations are important stakeholders in health care. There are various types of NGOs that support health-care organizations, such as community-based organizations and faith-based organizations. These organizations are trusted by communities and ensure the effective delivery of health care to marginalized communities.

Because of their reputation, these organizations are more influential as compared to government institutions associated with health care. In most cases, they are also equipped with the resources and infrastructure required to deliver effective health-care services.

5. Media agencies

Other stakeholders for health care include media and communication agencies. These agencies are owned by the government, private or nonprofit organizations. These organizations use radio, television, social media, artists, bloggers, journalists and PR professionals to spread health awareness to remote areas and engage marginalized communities in health-care programs. These agencies often work with NGOs to spread awareness regarding a health-care program or safety measures to prevent diseases.

6. Research institutes and universities

Research institutes and universities also serve as major stakeholders in health care. These institutes collate social and epidemiological data to design strategies that improve the delivery of health-care services. They also play an effective role in promoting health-related awareness by holding seminars and similar programs on university campuses.

7. Private sector

The private sector is a major stakeholder when it comes to health care. Many private companies believe in giving back to the community. For example, a hand sanitizer manufacturer may donate its products to nonprofit health-care organizations, or a sanitary napkin brand could donate products to eliminate period poverty.

These actions not only benefit patients but also create brand awareness for the products donated. This makes the private sector an instrumental partner in improving the delivery of health-care services.

8. Community members

Community members are as important as any other stakeholders when it comes to health care. Community members should be familiar with local-level health-care services. Health-care organizations can collaborate with community groups, such as women's groups and youth groups, to promote awareness regarding various health issues and disease prevention.

Community and local leaders support these groups. Since these groups are community representatives, health-care organizations can turn to them to learn about marginalized communities' problems. By collaborating with these groups, health-care organizations can tailor their services according to their audiences' demands.

Two-way communication can make it easier for health-care teams to understand the needs and perceptions of the community.

9. Infection prevention stakeholders

According to the Duty of Care law, health-care workers' responsibility is to prevent harm to themselves, their colleagues, patients and visitors. They are bound by rules and regulations that prevent the spread of diseases through equipment, physical contact and the health-care facility where patients or visitors are accommodated. Special cleaning protocols are introduced to ensure the creation of a safe space for workers and patients.

10. Internal stakeholders

The people working within a health-care organization are the internal stakeholders. They have stakes in the results of health-care projects. Most of the internal stakeholders who work for or within the health-care setup include administrators, management, employees and internal clients.

These individuals are committed to serving the organization they are working for. They are hired as staff, board members, volunteers and donors.

11. External stakeholders

The community members who are impacted by the services provided by a health-care organization, such as clients and community partners, are known as external stakeholders. The perspective of both internal and external stakeholders is necessary for the creation of an effective health-care system.

12. Patients' experience stakeholders

Patients' experience stakeholders include everyone from nurses to researchers, nursing educators, government, individual nurses, physicians, professional associations and more. These stakeholders are responsible for ensuring that patients receive the care they deserve.

Participation in Activities to Identify Innovative Solutions

To satisfy patients in the twenty-first century, health-care organizations should introduce policies and solutions that improve education, diagnosis, research quality and health-care access. The introduction of the latest technology can improve every aspect of health care, from simplifying information exchanges between patients and doctors to introducing robotics to make high-risk surgeries successful.

Some of the innovative solutions recently introduced in health care include:

Online consultations

Online consultations have made it easier to access health care. People can download various mobile applications on their phones to book appointments and schedule online consultations with specialists. Health-care organizations can register with these apps to access a wider population.

VR/AR in health care

VR and AR technology offers a multisensory experience that makes it easier for medical professionals to understand their patients' conditions. This immersive experience is used to prevent misdiagnosis.

Nanomedicine

Nanotechnology and nano-devices are transforming the health-care industry by improving control of health care at the molecular level. Nano-pharmaceutical companies aim to create precise delivery systems and nano-drugs, which are highly focused and target tumors rather than affecting the entire body.

3D printing

3D printing is taking the medical industry by the storm. It uses buildable materials, such as plastic and aluminum, to create medical tools. The custom-friendly aspect of 3D printing technology has made it possible to repair tissues, transplant organs and make braces, prosthetics and stem-cell organoids. Poly-pill development is one of the most groundbreaking results of 3D printing. It contains various drugs with different release times for multiple illnesses.

Internet of medical things

Access to patients' information is important in health care. Due to technological innovations, better ways to deal with and secure information regarding a patient have been introduced. Cloud computing and other connected devices have made the exchange of data easier. Health-care organizations can use the Internet of Things to keep a record of inventory and patients' data. It can also be used to monitor patients' health and provide them with preventive care.

The introduction of this technology has laid the foundation for various other tech advancements.

Precision medicine

Precision medicine reduces total treatment time. Doctors prescribe these medicines based on the results of diagnostic and genetic testing. These procedures include DNA mutation investigations and genome sequencing. This technology has revolutionized treatment, diagnosis and preventive care by offering tailored services that match patients' requirements and lifestyles. It is a major shift from the traditional approach to treatment.

Provide Consultation to Governing Bodies and Clinical Staff Regarding Their Roles

A health-care organization must consult its employees if they are affected by situations that involve their health. It should provide its staff the opportunity to express their concerns and contribute to decisions regarding their safety and protection.

All employees should be involved in discussions regarding a change of equipment or introductions of new risk-control policies. Employees should also be included in conversations related to the competence of facilities.

Listed below are some of the situations when health-care organization must consult their workers.

- Risk assessment
- Identification of hazards
- Controlling or eliminating risks
- Updating or changing workspace facilities
- Introducing changes that affect the safety and health of employees
- Decisions regarding employee safety, health, information and training.

Chapter 4: The Role of External Best Practices

What Are Best Practices?

Best practices are strategies and tactics employed by high-performing health-care organizations to improve their functional aspects. By implementing best practices, organizations can ensure that their practitioners and staff perform to their best potential, both efficiently and profitably.

There are two types of best practices introduced in a health-care organization:

- Internal best practices
- External best practices.

Internal Best Practices

Internal best practices are introduced by the people working in an organization. Sometimes various areas, units or functions perform better than the others. To improve an organization's overall performance, it is important to identify the practices that make these top performers better than the rest.

Once these practices are identified, they should be applied all across the organization for quality improvement. These practices will dramatically improve the entire organization's performance.

Apart from enhancing efficiency, identifying best practices can unveil remarkable creativity and innovation within the company. There are various benefits of leveraging internal best practices across an organization. Not only do they enhance the performance of an organization, but they also save money in the long run.

In addition to increased performance, the process of finding best practices breeds tremendous innovation and creativity.

Some companies use internal best practices as a standard for recruiting new employees. This allows organizations to both hire competitive candidates and retain hardworking employees longer than their competitors.

External Best Practices

Sometimes health-care organizations need to outsource services if they want to employ best practices.

As the name indicates, external best practices are applied to an organization's internal infrastructure that grows beyond its original structure. From production to customer care, each aspect of running a business can be improved by deploying external best practices.

The Purpose of External Best Practices

Sometimes companies need to look beyond their settings to find a solution to the problems they are facing. That's where the need to deploy external best practices arises. Organizations can hire change agents from other companies to implement these practices or learn from their competitors' success. Implementing external best practices means simplifying and streamlining organizational functions to produce the best results.

In some cases, complex changes need to be implemented. The aim is to reduce errors and mistakes and ensure that the organization runs faster, smoother and more efficiently. After identifying external best practices, companies need to create a plan to deploy them to achieve the best results. This plan serves as the framework for success. It also minimizes failures that slow down the progress of a business.

Implementation of External Best Practices

Once external best practices have been identified, it is time to implement them. Organizations need to create a plan they can stick to, to ensure that these practices are effectively implemented and followed. These practices will help them stand out from the crowd.

Various organizational factors help companies implement external best practices. These factors include effective communication, supportive organizational culture and the absorptive capacity of the organization. The stronger the existing structure, the easier it will be to implement external best practices.

Why Is the Implementation of External Best Practices Necessary?

Sharing best practices in an organization benefits it in a variety of ways:

Fosters a culture that promotes learning

For an organization to grow, it is important to create an environment that promotes learning. Implementing external best practices requires knowledge and awareness of advanced tools and technologies, such as social media and information-sharing platforms. To meet these demands, employees need to learn these skills. Therefore, by leveraging these technologies in its functions, a business can attract more clients and talented employees.

These technologies make it easier for a business to adapt to the ever-evolving market and enhance its employees' performance.

Identifies areas that require improvement

To achieve success, every organization needs to identify gaps that hinder its productivity. The implementation of external best practices helps managers identify and fill these knowledge gaps. It helps them design strategies that promote productivity and creativity in an organization, which increases the productivity of employees and streamlines business processes.

Generates creative ideas

The deployment of external best practices in an organization creates a culture that promotes innovative and creative ideas. It promotes critical thinking, which improves the organization's overall productivity and performance.

Helps make better decisions

Every business wants to keep its customers happy. Organizations need to quickly adopt practices that solve the problems their customers face. The implementation of external best practices makes every process, including decision-making, easier. This improves the organization's image, productivity and performance.

Adds to competence and efficiency

Deploying external best practices gives employees a road map to follow. As they do not waste their time figuring out what they need to do to achieve the desired outcomes, they can use this newly available time to work on the more important aspects of running the organization. This increases productivity and efficiency.

Implementing external best practices reduces the time it takes to achieve the expected results because employees know where to look for the desired information. When they have a definite route to follow, employees can share their perspectives and ideas in a relaxed environment. This improves the productivity of the company.

Building a supportive work environment

To build and strengthen bonds between employees, managers need to form a close-knit community within an organization. They need to leverage the right platforms that make it easier to share information. These platforms also provide a secure and authentic way to save information. This information can be accessed only by authenticated users and is shared consistently when necessary.

Accessing the internal knowledge base

We live in a world where everyone can share their opinion on social media. This makes it even more important to satisfy customers as much as possible. One of the most important features of good customer service is a quick response to customer queries.

This makes it important for customer service representatives to have access to an internal knowledge base. This knowledge base will keep them up to date with an organization's policies, techniques and practices. This allows customer service representatives to provide customers with the information they need on time, which improves the organization's image and allows it to retain its consumers.

Managing the loss of information

One of the biggest assets that any organization possesses is its critical information. The loss of this knowledge can wreak havoc on a company. Therefore, this information needs to be effectively managed and secured.

Achieving cost and time efficiency

External best practices are tried and tested before they are implemented. Additionally, introducing best practices in an organization can save employees from committing mistakes due to lack of experience. Employees know what they need to do and when. This saves time and money needed to fix mistakes later on.

Customer representatives also have a set route to follow to address customers' concerns. This set route can help them improve customer experience because it allows the representatives to make the right response at the right time.

Examples of Implementation of Best Practices

The following organizations have correctly implemented best practices:

AHRQ

The AHRQ divides the process of implementation of best practices into three stages:

Managing staff

In the first stage, roles and responsibilities are assigned to:

- Members of the team
- Unit-based team members
- Team leaders.

Updating work organization

- Identifying paths of reporting and ongoing communication
- Leveraging processes to address accountability
- Identifying practices to build new routines and improve existing routines.

Adding best practices to operations

- Refining a preliminary implementation plan
- Assuring support from key stakeholders
- Devising a plan to test newly added best practices
- Establishing practices to engage staff
- Helping employees learn new practices by creating education plans.

IHI

IHI took the following route to implement best practices in their organization:

Plan to improve performance

Strategizing to improve employees' performance, processes and operations is the first thing to be done before implementing best practices. For that, managers need to identify the gaps that affect overall organizational performance. Once these gaps are identified, core measures are devised. These measures are implemented for all employees, improving their performance and productivity.

These measures are implemented to streamline the following operations:

- Identifying patients
- Conducting interventions in case of missed elements of care bundles
- Educating staff
- Reporting barriers and outliers that impair care quality.

Strive for consistency

Quality improvement on an organizational level requires aware staff and patients. The higher patient literacy levels are, the easier it is to communicate with them.

Organizations have to face various problems when it comes to educating patients and employees. However, staying consistent is key.

It is crucial to keep employees up to date with the latest information and technologies related to health care. It is also important to organize health promotion programs so patients better understand their treatment plans and cooperate with health-care professionals.

Develop ongoing processes

Educating staff is an ongoing process. With the rise of new technology, seemingly every day, new processes and technologies are being introduced within the health-care sector, all of which are hard to keep pace with. To excel, every organization needs to constantly improve its best practices by using the right technology for quality improvement.

WHO

WHO best practices require the application of several tenets:

Effectiveness

All best practices that are implemented should be effective and must produce measurable results.

Efficiency

To be deployed, best practices must offer the desired results within a reasonable period. They should utilize a moderate level of resources.

Relevance

Any practice that has to be deployed should prioritize health problems, such as problems faced by the African continent.

Ethical soundness

Best practices should align with said and unsaid ethical considerations that deal with the human population.

Sustainability

The proposed practice should be sustainable—it should work for the organization for a long period.

Duplication

Best practices should be customizable and replicable in other organizations or other parts of the country.

Partnerships

The proposed practices must allow collaboration between various stakeholders.

Community involvement

Affected communities must be actively involved in the process of proposing best practices.

Political commitment

The proposed practice should be supported by local and national authorities.

The Takeaway from These Organizations

Building a community is vital to an organization's success. Implementation of best practices can make that happen. They improve the flow of information within the company and ensure that every problem is solved on time.

Most external best practices are tried and tested before implementation, making the chances of errors low. These practices enhance employee efficiency and productivity. They save money and time and make organizational operations more transparent.

Chapter: 5 Methods to Improve Quality in Health Care

The Importance of Improving Quality in Health Care

With the advent of technology, medical science has advanced tremendously; however, there is still room for improving patient safety and addressing patient needs. Today's health-care systems perform far below acceptable levels; these systems need to be improved.

Access to the internet and better data conservation techniques have slowly replaced the traditional practices of using memory, pen and paper to write reports. Physicians have to deal with hundreds of patients daily, so it is crucial to have an advanced system that keeps patient records consolidated in one place to improve care.

The quality of health-care services can be significantly improved by deliberately redesigning health-care systems to make them more efficient, inexpensive and sustainable. The integration of specialized tools and methods is required to make this change.

Health-care systems should use intuitive software that keeps electronic medical records. This software can lay the foundation for a user-centric design for health-care spaces. This can make the process of providing health-care services timelier and more reliable. Well-designed health-care systems can also afford health-care workers more time to improve services.

Accelerated Performance with an Improved Health-Care System

Just like any other organization, health-care institutions require a systematic approach to operate efficiently and systematically. This approach includes close monitoring, improvement and assessment of health care provided to patients. The purpose of introducing this approach into the system is to reach the highest possible performance level slowly but steadily.

Health processes can be made more efficient and streamlined by implementing methodologies, including:

- Practice management systems
- Patient engagement
- Care coordination software.

How Can the Quality of the Health-Care System Be Improved?

There are some principles health-care organizations must consider if they wish to achieve the highest level of performance possible. A successful organizational health-care system depends on its efficiency, service delivery approach, consumer satisfaction and reliable results. Listed below are the principles that should be considered in order to improve the quality of health-care systems.

Creating processes and systems

Every health-care organization is different and requires the development of systems and processes that meet its specific needs. No matter the organization's size, the quality improvement approach should be introduced to simplify "Input – Process – Output." This approach should align with the organization's needs and culture.

Patient-centered quality improvement approach

The key to improving health-care processes is to implement a patient-centered business strategy. The desired level of performance should be based on patient needs and expectations. For that, health-care professionals must identify what patients expect. This information will serve as the foundation of systems and processes that improve health-care services. These improvements should be made while considering:

- Evidence-based care
- Patient safety
- Patient engagement
- Health literacy
- Communication centered on the patient literacy level
- Systems to support patient access.

Use data for quality improvement

Data is the key to quality improvement because it provides health-care organizations with the information they need to update their systems and processes. It helps them figure out how their current system works and makes it easier for them to monitor and compare the trend data of existing processes and systems. Data-driven insights improve health-care quality by providing more accurate results, fewer readmissions, minimum medical errors and low infection rates.

To improve the quality of health-care services, both qualitative and quantitative data need to be collected.

Allow care coordination

The coordination of care activities is important when medical professionals are dealing with patients who have chronic conditions. It makes the transition between health-care providers easier by reducing care fragmentation and ensuring effective communication between providers for effective referrals.

Development of Quality Structures

Quality improvement of the health-care system requires the development of quality structures that monitor the activities and processes within a health-care system. The success of a health-care organization depends upon the multitude of systems and disciplines integrated into it.

Formation of committees

To make these systems work most effectively, the development of quality improvement teams or committees is required. These committees include people who carry out and monitor improvement efforts.

An effective quality improvement committee includes professionals from multiple areas of practice. Each of these areas will be affected by the implementation of the proposed improvement. Patient representatives should also be a part of this committee because they can communicate the patients' needs, concerns, demands and expectations as clearly as possible.

The quality improvement committee meets regularly to propose improvements based on collected data and identify areas with room for improvement. Once these proposals are approved, the team's job is to implement them.

There are a variety of tools and models used to identify the weaknesses of a health-care system. These QI tools and approaches include:

- Model for Improvement (MFI)
- Audits
- Benchmarking
- Workflow mapping, assessments
- Plan-Do-Study-Act (PDSA) cycles
- Best practices research
- Feedback.

The leader of the team should be a health-care professional who is committed to continuously upgrading the system. The leader should propose approaches and practices that pave the way for constant improvement and implement these practices to enable ongoing improvement.

Quality improvement practices encompass data collection, reviewing the data collected, identifying best practices and encouraging team members to share their perspectives on all aspects of the health-care system. Under the supervision of the right leader, the committee will work efficiently and enable the organization to achieve the highest performance level possible.

Innovation of councils

Health system councils are strategic alliances formed from the plethora of health systems operating in a region. The purpose of these councils is to offer guidance to health companies. They consist of professionals with years of experience in all areas of medical practice.

The formation of these councils keeps health-care organizations on the same page. They provide guidance the organizations need to innovate their systems with the latest tech processes.

Setting strategic goals helps health-care product manufacturers seek new product opportunities that improve a region's health-care system. The top priority of these councils is to bring innovation to the systems and pave the way for a new health-care age.

Development of Data Management Systems

Due to the advent of technology, health-care data has become increasingly digitalized. In this age of technological advancement, data management systems have become an important need of every industry. Health care is no exception, as data created by health-care organizations is constantly growing both in terms of volume and value.

Health data management systems make it easier to process and manage this ever-increasing data. The development and incorporation of data management systems benefit everyone, including health-care organizations, health-care professionals and patients.

Databases and Their Use

A well-structured health-care database system is essential. By incorporating the right technology, health-care providers can improve the quality of services.

Software to keep electronic health records

The most important step that has to be taken to improve health-care processes is to introduce patient-centered health record software. These records make it more efficient and accurate to track a patient's treatment. Electronic health records are an advanced and safer way to save clinical data. The incorporation of such software streamlines health-care processes and offers more reliable outcomes.

The uses of databases

- They improve a health-care system's efficiency by offering easy access to accurate and up-to-date patients' information.
- They make the exchange of information smoother.
- They allow effective monitoring and improvement of health care.
- They make it easier to assess the current systems in place.
- They help track health-care usage.
- They secure patients' critical health information.
- They eliminate medical errors and make prescriptions and diagnoses easier.
- They improve the interaction between health-care providers and patients.
- They make billing and documentation easier.
- They reduce the cost of paperwork and hiring of clerical staff, which eventually reduces the cost of running the medical facility.

Registries and their importance

A patient registry is the record of a patient's medical history and personal information. In most cases, patient registries are disease-specific. They help researchers find the root of the problem or the incidence of disease.

Patient registries help researchers accurately estimate how a particular disease survives and also allows them to identify its natural history. This enables researchers to find answers to how many people currently have a disease, what its symptoms are and how severe the illness is.

The information acquired through these registries improves the level of performance and health-care services. It enables health-care professionals to provide more accurate advice to patients for effective treatment and quick recovery. This information also adds to patients' life expectancy, even when the cure of a disease is unknown.

Facilitation of change

One of the most important characteristics of modern health-care organizations is the facilitation of change—the organizational change that aligns changes in people's values, behaviors and aspirations with changes in systems, processes and strategies.

A well-planned approach is required to introduce changes in a health-care organization. These organizations require a facilitator who will look for opportunities to improve and create successful strategies that make required changes possible.

Conducting population health promotion activities

Health promotion programs are designed to make individuals and communities aware of an unhealthy lifestyle's risks and hazards. These programs encourage people to adopt healthy habits and change their lifestyles to manage the risk of chronic diseases.

Health promotion activities make the following processes easier:

Handoff

A handoff is a way of transferring the information, responsibility and authority of a patient from one health-care provider to another.

Transition of care

Transition of care is a well-planned transfer of young adults with chronic diseases from children-oriented to adult-oriented health-care systems.

Episode of care

The entire treatment based on an episode of illness is known as an episode of care.

Outcomes

Outcome management is referred to as managing the gaps in patient care, identifying patients at risk and improving health-care provision on multiple levels in an organization.

Health-care utilization

Health-care utilization is the measure of services utilized to prevent and treat health problems, maintain good health and collect information regarding a patient's prognosis and health status.

Chapter 6: Change Theories in Health Care

One of the biggest challenges health-care organizations have to overcome is dealing with change. Complex health-care organizations deal with multiple challenges daily, including managing health-care costs, introducing new technology, managing workforce shortages and caring for an increasingly elderly population. Each of these aspects serves as a force that drives the change in a hospital or clinic.

With the advent of technology and advanced medical science, health-care organizations must constantly change to keep pace with the ever-evolving medical world. They need to upgrade systems and processes to deliver the highest-quality services and ensure patient and employee satisfaction. This is important not only to generate business but to retain employees.

Introducing changes in a health-care organization is a big challenge. There are various factors that affect the outcomes of change:

- The content of change
- The change process
- The organization where the change needs to be implemented
- The people working within an organization.

Types of Changes in a Health-Care Organization

There are two types of changes that take place in a health-care organization:

- Planned change
- Change by drift.

When nature runs its course without external interference, the change that takes place is referred to as the drift method. No single person has any control over this form of change, nor is there any effort to bring about this change because it is often accidental.

In contrast, a planned change has a purpose and intention behind it. Planned changes require strong leadership and the competence to implement said changes organization-wide. Leaders must have knowledge and skills in various areas of practice in a health-care organization.

Rather than questioning whether they should intervene in the natural flow of events, organizations today are planning for change and its ramifications.

The needs and expectations of people are the drivers of change. Over time, the needs of the population that requires medical care grow. Integrating the right technology in the systems will make it easier to manage these needs and provide satisfactory health-care services. To do this, health-care organizations must identify which areas need improvement. This will help them effectively plan, manage and implement the necessary changes.

The Purpose of Change Models

Change models are composed of theories, concepts and methodologies required to bring an in-depth change to a health-care organization. Change models serve as a guide to make changes. They also help monitor the transformation process to ensure that the required changes are effectively implemented and practiced. No matter who these changes apply to, change management frameworks or models make it easier to implement and maintain them.

The Change Agent

The change agent is an individual who is adept at the implementation of the theory of change. The change agent's ability to put a theory into practice plays a vital role in successfully improving health-care service quality.

It is the responsibility of the change agent to balance every aspect of running a health-care organization. In most situations, the change agent is an internal source or the manager of the organization. However, in other cases, external sources are hired. Some of the best attributes of a change agent include:

- Guiding people toward change
- Being a role model to colleagues
- Inspiring change in colleagues
- Allowing the facilitation of change.

Change agents supervise the overall process of change. They offer constant support to their colleagues and also provide feedback to management based on the results obtained by the facilitation of the change.

Implementing a change theory is often complicated and challenging. Successful facilitation of change brings a sense of achievement and pride. Conversely, unsuccessful implementation of change may distress employees.

It is the responsibility of change agents to deal with how employees are feeling. They should use their knowledge and skills according to the situation at hand, ensuring that change is not impaired by staff resistance. This action requires exceptional communication skills and the ability to build strong relationships.

Change agents must evaluate how the change needs to be implemented and should be able to plan accordingly. It should also be kept in mind that hiring a skilled change agent is not the only factor that influences the implementation of effective change in the organization—various other factors also play their part in the process.

Types of Change Models and Theories

It is human nature to resist change, but change is important for any organization to grow. A change management model serves as a compass that helps health-care providers make the navigation process easier. It guides change agents on how to get their entire team on the same page.

A change management model helps a health-care organization prepare to deal with resistance. It makes the change easier by guiding the entire team toward success.

Change Management Models

Every health-care organization has different goals in mind. The choice of model depends upon the needs of the business and its culture. For some organizations, large-scale models work best, whereas, for others, less complex models may be more suitable.

Listed below are some tried-and-tested change management models that have been used to implement effective changes in a health-care organization.

1. Lewin's Change Management Model

Kurt Lewin developed this three-phase change model. Its purpose is to break down a complex change into smaller, more manageable parts, which are:

- Unfreeze
- Change
- Refreeze.

The first step when orchestrating a change in an organization is to analyze your current systems and processes. The first step of Lewin's change model asks the change agent to unfreeze the current organizational process to identify the areas that need improvement. This helps everyone working in an organization understand the need for change.

The next step is to implement the change. The change agent must guide everyone affected by the change throughout the process. Once the change model is deployed, the system needs to be solidified or refrozen and brought into practice.

Lewin's change model can be personalized to the needs of an organization. It can be used with both simple and complex health-care organizations. The change phase can be further divided into various parts to deal with resistance and make it easier for employees to accept these changes.

Senior management can use this model in an organization to implement team-wide or organization-wide changes.

2. McKinsey 7-S Model

The McKinsey 7-S Model is used by organizations that want to bring complex changes to their organizational structure. Each element of this model affects the other, making it easier for change agents to identify the loopholes in health-care organizations' structures, processes and systems.

The seven elements of the McKinsey 7-S Model are:

- Strategy
- Structure
- Systems
- Shared values
- Style
- Staff
- Skills.

The seven elements of this model are divided into two groups. The first three elements are referred to as the "hard elements," whereas the rest are considered "soft elements." Improving strategy, structure and systems within an organization requires a lot of planning and hard work. Hence, these are considered hard elements.

Conversely, the other four elements are more fluid and depend on work culture. Hence they are referred to as soft elements. For successful implementation of this model, balancing all aspects and understanding how these affect one other is important.

This framework is ideal for situations where the problem needs to be identified within an organization. Once the issue is identified, it can be addressed in a timely manner.

3. Nudge theory

Nudge theory depends on evidence-based indirect or subtle suggestions that encourage employees to accept change. The concept behind this change management model is that nudging changes are more widely accepted compared to strictly enforced changes.

To understand and implement this theory, some basic principles need to be considered:

- Defining the change
- Understanding the employees' point of view
- Offering evidence to support suggestions and options
- Suggesting change as a choice rather than an order
- Valuing employee feedback
- Keeping options limited
- Using short-term wins to solidify the change.

Nudge theory enables employees to see and understand the need for change. It makes them more accepting of the organization-wide change, which will influence the way they work. Implementing this model reduces resistance and makes it easier to improve the quality of health-care services.

4. The ADKAR Change Management Model

The ADKAR change model is centered on the people behind the change. It is an acronym, and each letter represents a goal that needs to be achieved by implementing this model.

This acronym can be broken down into parts, which are:

- Awareness (the reason the change is required)
- Desire (support and participation needed to make change implementation a success)
- Knowledge (what needs to be changed and how)
- Ability (expertise and skill needed to effectively implement the change)
- Reinforcement (making sustainable changes).

This model focuses on employees. Like nudge theory, this model also encourages employee participation and support in implementing the change. Change agents make their peers aware of the need for change and help them understand how they will benefit from its implementation. This way, the ADKAR Model ensures everyone working within an organization is on the same page.

5. Kübler-Ross Change Curve

As mentioned earlier, it is human nature to resist change. Health-care organizations should understand that they will sometimes have to deal with emotional reactions instead of logic-based objections in response to change. When change is introduced in an organization, employees experience these five stages:

1. Denial
2. Anger
3. Bargaining
4. Depression
5. Acceptance.

To effectively implement change, a health-care organization needs to empathize and understand employees' emotional state. This helps management gain the support of the employees because employees realize that the organization values their emotions.

This model works best for small organizations rather than those that require large-scale changes.

6. Bridges' Transition Model

This model is similar to the Kübler-Ross Change Curve. It also focuses on the emotions of those involved in the process of change. This theory breaks the process down into three stages:

- Ending, losing and letting go
- The neutral zone
- The new beginning.

According to this theory, change happens to everyone who wants to achieve a higher goal. The organization should be prepared to deal with any outburst that comes in response to the change. This will make it easier to guide team members to the neutral zone and eventually help them embark on a new journey.

Chapter 7: Statutory and Regulatory Requirements

Define Statutory and Regulatory

What are statutory obligations?

The current laws passed by the state or federal government are referred to as statutory obligations. In most cases, these obligations are static and do not change unless new laws are passed; however, statutory laws need to be updated in other cases. The best example is the HITECH Act that updated the 20-year-old HIPAA laws.

What are regulatory obligations?

Regulatory obligations are legal requirements through proxy. The regulating body appointed by the government issues and regulates the requirements. Unlike statutory obligations, regulatory obligations change often.

Both statutory and regulatory obligations must be complied with—this is nonnegotiable. If an organization fails to comply with these legal requirements, it is charged a penalty or fine. In some cases, such offenses can result in a custodial sentence of the individuals who are responsible for the failure.

What Are Statutory and Regulatory Requirements?

CMS Compliance

Health-care organizations need to comply with various statutory and regulatory requirements to avoid fines and penalties. They must establish Medicare compliance programs to ensure their operations comply with and adhere to Centers for Medicare & Medicaid Services' (CMS) standards. These programs serve as a framework for health-care organizations. They help them assess their performance and aid them in trying to improve it within the boundaries of the law.

These programs are designed to achieve the following goals:

- Prevent noncompliance
- Detect noncompliance
- Correct noncompliance
- Prevent fraud, abuse and waste of resources.

The Medicare compliance department in a health-care organization ensures that every aspect of the organization is working in compliance with CMS statutory and regulatory obligations. The Medicare compliance department works with the following departments of a health-care organization:

Ethics and compliance

This department creates and maintains codes of business conduct and oversees the process of disclosure of conflicts of interest.

External audit and investigation

This department deals with the detection, correction and prevention of external fraud.

Human resources

This department is responsible for enforcing disciplinary standards.

Privacy and security

This department secures and maintains both electronic and nonelectronic records of patients' personal health information.

Internal audit and investigation

This department is responsible for ensuring and auditing internal operations to ensure compliance within an organization.

How Does CMS Compliance Need to Be Implemented All Across the Organization?

Medicare compliance programs need to be effectively implemented at all levels of the organization. This implementation requires participation from all employees. These programs should encourage staff members to:

Follow policies and procedures

Managers should effectively communicate policies and procedures to employees. Employees should know where to easily find the policies and procedures relevant to their jobs. Staff members should also be provided with a clear description of their workflow.

Engage in training

Employees who are involved in the administration process or the delivery of Medicare benefits should be professionally trained. There should be a set of obligations they comply with. If new staff is hired, they should be trained within 90 days of the day they were hired. Managers should be prepared to deal with the new employees' compliance risks based on their organizational roles.

Know how to access resources

Employees working within a health-care organization should be familiar with the appropriate resources they need to perform to their best potential. These resources include:

- CMS manuals
- Department-specific procedures and policies
- Medicare complaint department.

The supervisor of the Medicare compliance programs should always be available to address employees' concerns.

Audit and monitor operational areas

Employees should be encouraged to fully cooperate with the process of monitoring and auditing operational areas. This step is crucial to ensure effective compliance all across the organization.

Report noncompliance

Employees should feel safe reporting noncompliance, fraud, ethical, privacy and abuse issues by the organization itself. If employees identify noncompliance, they should immediately report it to the Medicare complaint department. A special framework should be put in place to ensure these issues are reported and dealt with on time.

HIPAA Compliance

Every health-care organization must comply with standards set by the Health Insurance Portability and Accountability Act (HIPAA). HIPAA protects patients' sensitive personal data. HIPAA regulates companies that deal with health care. These companies must introduce HIPAA compliance programs that protect health information through security, network and physical measures.

Entities covered by HIPAA include:

- Treatment providers
- Payers
- Operations and processes in a health-care organization.

Business associates who need to comply with HIPAA obligations include:

- People who have access to patient information
- People who help with patient treatment, operation and payment.

Each of these groups needs to meet HIPAA compliance. In some instances, subcontractors and other similar business associates also come under the HIPAA compliance rule. They should maintain compliance to protect critical patient information.

HIPAA Privacy and Security Rules

HIPAA sets standards to protect patients' health information. Per Health and Human Services (HHS), it is important to secure the Identifiable Health Information of a patient to ensure privacy. HIPAA sets standards to protect this information.

The HIPAA Security Rule establishes standards that protect patients' critical health information in an electronic form. The Civil Rights Department, working under HHS, regulates privacy and security rules by enforcing civil monetary penalties and voluntary compliance.

Why is HIPAA compliance required?

We live in a technology-driven world where any information can be accessed in a matter of minutes. More than ever, health-care organizations are adopting computerized operations, such as Electronic Health Records (EHR) and computerized physician order entry (CPOE) systems, to implement HIPAA compliance programs.

When signing up for health-care plans, people are required to provide their personal health information. Even though leveraging technology in health care has improved data mobility and efficiency, it has also increased security risks. Therefore, every organization needs to put security rules in place. These rules ensure that the privacy of an individual's health information is not violated. They also provide health-care professionals with a framework to follow, which can improve the quality of services provided.

Security rules can be personalized to the size, needs and organizational structure of a company. They can also be customized to the risks to patients' e-PHI.

Physical and technical safeguards for HIPAA compliance

Health-care organizations put various physical and technical safeguards in place to ensure effective HIPAA compliance. These safeguards are proposed by HHS, which regulates HIPAA compliance. Organizations that host critical patient data must put strict security rules in place. Some of the physical safeguards proposed by HHS include:

- Limited and authorized access to sensitive patient information
- Strict and clear policies regarding the use of workstations and access to digital media
- Special monitoring of actions such as transfer, disposal, removal and reuse of electronic media and electronic PHI
- Technical safeguards to ensure that only authorized individuals can access patients' health information (listed below are some of the technical safeguards imposed by HIPAA)
- The use of unique user IDs, encryption, decryption, automatic logging off and access procedures in an emergency
- Reporting and monitoring of hardware and software activity with the help of logs and audit reports.

Data protection strategies

The need for data security has increased more than ever before. Organizations are adopting electronic means to share and record data. To provide top-quality care, health-care organizations are leveraging technology to meet the growing demand for data. However, they need HIPAA compliance programs to protect and maintain PHI.

By having a well-developed data strategy in place, health-care organizations can achieve the following goals:

- Maintain the trust of patients and health-care providers by ensuring the protection and availability of PHI
- Meet HITECH and HIPAA regulations while accessing, controlling, auditing, transmitting and securing data
- Acquire more control over sensitive organizational data and maintain greater visibility.

OSHA Compliance

OSHA compliance means adhering to all regulations devised to make the workplace safer. Maintaining OSHA compliance reduces the spread of diseases and injuries within an organization. OSHA standards must be followed by both government and public health-care organizations. Some of these standards include:

- Employers must provide a hazard-free workspace. Standard rules and regulations issued by OSHA should be followed.
- Employees should be provided with PPE that ensures complete protection and which fits the employees it is intended for.
- Workers should be aware of the potential hazards in a workspace. Organizations should use safety signs, posters, labels and color codes as appropriate.
- Organizations should ensure the use of safe and well-maintained tools and equipment in the workplace.
- Employees must be educated about their rights to a safe workplace. Employers should place an OSHA poster in an area where it is prominent and visible to all.
- Employees who file complaints should not be punished, experience retaliation or be discriminated against.
- Employers should correct OSHA noncompliance as soon as possible. Citations issued by inspectors should be posted in the area where noncompliance took place.
- Employees' access to illness- and work-related injury logs should be maintained.
- All employees should be safety-trained in a language that they easily understand.
- Businesses must develop, foster and update operating procedures and communicate them to employees.

PPACA Compliance

With the advent of technology, the HR marketplace is constantly evolving. PPACA serves as a framework for employers to stay up to date with health-care reforms. This makes it easier for employers and employees to understand health coverage. The PPACA framework introduces various laws and rules that companies have to comply with if they wish to offer health-care benefits. It makes health coverage more affordable for employees, and they can get subsidies, cost-sharing reductions and premium tax credits because of it.

Why should health-care organizations switch to SaaS technology for PPACA compliance?

Most health-care organizations use payroll/HRIS/benefits-administration platforms based on SaaS technology, or the cloud. These platforms are easy to update after PPACA requirements are released.

Organizations that use older platforms or software often face compliance roadblocks because older software impairs communication. Therefore, switching to SaaS technology is important for employers.

Goals of PPACA

PPACA is also known as ACA or Obamacare. It is a comprehensive health-care reform law created to achieve three main goals:

- Ensure the availability of affordable health insurance for all. It offers subsidies to low-income households.
- Cover low-income adults with Medicaid programs. This program has not yet been expanded to all states.
- Lower the general cost of health care by promoting innovative medical care delivery methods.

Chapter 8: Accreditation, Certification and Recognition

Defining Accreditation, Certification and Recognition

Accreditation

The International Society for Quality in Healthcare states that accreditation is a process in which external peers evaluate the compliance of an organization's performance standards with pre-established ones. Accreditation aims to improve upon existing quality standards through continuous improvement strategies rather than by forcing compliance.

Accreditation indicates that a center conforms to an agreed standard of excellence by conducting ongoing performance monitoring and assessment. Essentially, it shows how well a quality management system is working. This type of procedure ensures that all staff members' actions are carried out in full compliance with agreed-upon standards.

Certification

Certification entails individuals voluntarily giving up their time and energy to be evaluated by a third party, such as a nongovernmental agency. To join or be evaluated by this organization, volunteers must meet specific eligibility requirements and be assessed by the agency before being deemed "certified." An organization's compliance with set standards (e.g., ISO 9000) is formalized through external certification and evaluated by an auditor.

A certification is a designated credential earned by individuals to give them legitimacy and provide employers with assurances that they are qualified and competent to perform a job.

Recognition

In the health-care industry, organizations emphasize performance metrics linked to the Affordable Care Act in their reward and recognition programs to encourage employee engagement, reduce voluntary nursing staff turnover and drive employee loyalty.

Purpose of Accreditation, Certification and Recognition

Accreditation

Accreditation contributes to a greater level of confidence and faith in hospitals because it allows organizations to continually practice excellence while also performing in the best interest of all patients. Research has consistently shown that general accreditation programs lead to improved structure and care processes and strengthen care quality by improving clinical outcomes.

The primary purpose of accreditation is to ensure effective patient care standards, access to high-quality health care at affordable prices and safety in hospitals in all parts of the world. Through accreditation, programs can rectify deficiencies, leading to higher standards and greater professional responsibility.

Certification

Certification demonstrates an individual's commitment to the health-care profession. Nowadays, more and more employers are leveraging certification to determine which individuals possess the knowledge, skills and abilities required for success in a particular job role. They want to hire the best-qualified individuals who will significantly contribute to the quality of care patients receive.

Recognition

Organizations can build efficiency and job satisfaction by focusing on specific metrics with recognition initiatives. The impact of this activity is likely to yield positive effects. For example, it has been shown that people's productivity and work quality improve when they are engaged and motivated. Reinforcing and recognizing behaviors that support those values directly aligns organizations with the vision and mission they aspire to.

Options for Accreditation, Certification and Recognition

An accreditation source should be selected to fit an organization's mission, vision and culture. The accrediting source must match the organization's complexity, clinical focus and values.

Organizations can support their competitive edge by creating or maintaining performance metrics and recognition and incentive awards targeted toward organizational goals. Health-care staff recognition programs include awards that can be presented privately or publicly to recognize employees for various accomplishments.

Accreditation Association for Ambulatory Health Care (AAHC)

The Accreditation Association for Ambulatory Health Care has developed standards for patient safety and quality care in ambulatory health care and surgery centers, like private endoscopy suites. Since 1979, the Accreditation Association for Ambulatory Health Care (AAAHC) has been a privately held, not-for-profit organization aiming to provide higher standards of care.

Organizations cannot attain accreditation unless they demonstrate compliance with rigorous AAAHC standards. This standard is recognized as a symbol of excellence among third-party payers, medical organizations, liability insurance companies, state and federal agencies and the public. It demonstrates an organization's commitment to providing the highest-quality services to patients.

Commission on Accreditation of Rehabilitation Facilities (CARF)

An international nonprofit organization founded in 1966 by then-US Secretary of Social, Rehabilitation and Developmental Services Mary E. Switzer, CARF is a leader in international efforts in health and rehabilitation. It provides national and international accreditation services to facilities and programs.

With the support of CARF, organizations in the human services field help set standards and accredit individuals and departments globally and in institutions and facilities.

DNV GL

"Det Norske Veritas" (Norway) translates into "the Norwegian Truth," while "Germanischer Lloyd" is a trademark or trade name of Germanischer Lloyd (Germany). In September 2013, Germanischer Lloyd joined DNV to form DNV GL. They strive to improve patient safety and quality of care by ensuring hospital accreditation, managing infection risk and organizing system certification, clinical program certification and training.

Their goal is to enhance health-care quality and facilitate safe, patient-centered care by working with health-care providers, national and regional health authorities and other key stakeholders across the globe. The certification body is a world leader with objectives to safeguard life, property and the environment.

International Organization for Standardization (ISO)

The ISO is an independent international organization. ISO certification ensures that a quality control management system, manufacturing process, service or documentation procedure satisfies all the requirements for standardization and quality assurance.

An ISO standard is a written description of a specified level of quality, safety or efficiency specified for products, services and systems.

In ISO 9001, quality management is defined as following a series of quality management principles. This standard provides businesses and organizations with efficiency and customer satisfaction by conforming to many quality management principles.

If a company calls itself "ISO 9001 Certified," this means it has met all the requirements for certification established by the International Organization for Standardization (ISO 9001).

The Joint Commission

The Joint Commission is an independent accrediting and standard-setting organization that sets standards for the health-care industry. For more than six decades, the Joint Commission has provided standardized protocols for assessing health-care organizations based on their work's quality and safety.

The aim is to improve health care for the public, collaborate with other stakeholders, assess the health-care system and inspire organizations to provide the best care possible by improving safety, effectiveness and value.

The Joint Commission evaluates and accredits more than 17,000 health-care organizations in the United States. An independent review of performance by accreditation and certification assures the public of the quality and safety of services.

Baldrige

Health care and other industries have proven the Baldrige Criteria for Performance Excellence to be an effective guide for improving efficiency and solving complex problems. The Baldrige framework consists of seven interrelated criteria categories and scoring guidelines.

The Baldrige National Quality Award (MBNQA), established by the US Congress in 1987, is the nation's highest presidential award for performance excellence. This award recognizes companies that have implemented successful quality management systems.

Magnet

A Magnet Hospital Recognition Program for Excellence in Nursing Services was approved in December 1990 by the Board of Directors of the American Nurses Association (ANA). This project was based on a 1983 study by the American Academy of

Nursing that identified characteristics that help health-care organizations excel at recruiting and retaining nurses.

Organizations that earn Magnet Accreditation provide the highest level of nursing care, contribute to positive work environments and help shape future nursing profession changes. This program lays out a set of requirements for excellence in nursing care to benefit the entire organization.

An organization applying for Magnet status every four years must submit an annual report. Getting Magnet certification involves a lengthy and thorough evaluation process.

The Magnet Recognition Program offers nurses increased education and development that affords them increased autonomy. The Magnet Recognition Program also offers patients excellent care delivered by nurses who are supported to be the best they can be. Listed below are some benefits of Magnet accreditation:

- Best possible care for patients
- Financial success and company growth
- Motivation and value for staff.

Assisting of Survey and Accreditation Readiness

The accreditation process is voluntary and administered every three years as part of the Medicare survey. A health-care provider can elect to be accredited independently. Some states require accreditation for the initial assessment of home health and hospice patients.

A provider may choose to be accredited independently. Some states require accreditation for initial certification surveys for home health and hospice. Sometimes accreditation can be used instead of state license checks. Private providers of home health care and hospice programs may choose accreditation to demonstrate their organizations' excellence, especially accrediting requirements that are higher than the state licensure requirement and Medicare Conditions of Participation (CoPs).

The Accreditation Readiness Self-Assessment Tool is used to determine whether a program is accreditation-ready. It contains multiple-choice questions on each of the accreditation domains and standards and lets the organization assess whether its program meets them or not.

Health-care surveys can prove to be one of the most valuable sources of health-care accreditation information. The questionnaires let accrediting organizations know about a facility's various characteristics, including cleanliness, the quality of its communication system and overall care, among other variables.

Chapter 9: Evaluation of Compliance with Internal and External Requirements

Compliance means to obey and follow specific rules set out in regulations, specifications, standards or laws. Health-care compliance professionals are needed to address the ever-growing number of privacy and usage rules and regulations in health-care operations. Compliance programs regulate health-care organizations and help them maintain patient privacy and security, protect health-care staff, ensure quality patient care, prevent fraud and protect the health-care system.

A company's compliance program decreases the risk of fines, penalties, lawsuits and the shutdown of unauthorized activities or work stoppages. Failure to comply could lead to the closure of a company. There are two types of compliance regulations: internal and external.

Auditing and Monitoring

Monitoring and auditing are components of a health-care organization that allow it to identify areas that require improvement while simultaneously ensuring that the existing systems are free of errors.

A health-care audit is a systematic and objective approach aimed at evaluating and improving a Medicare compliance program's effectiveness. Its objective is to assess long-term monitoring practices and ensure that policies, procedures and control measures are adequate to reduce errors and risks.

Monitoring involves detecting compliance risks present in an organization's operations and striving to prevent them. Management should ensure internal processes and procedures are monitored so that changes in regulations and laws are complied with as soon as they are made. Necessary steps must be taken to monitor and verify that these guidelines are complied with.

What Are Internal and External Requirements?

The health-care sector is one of the most vital parts of the American industry. This importance necessitates health-care compliance, which can involve both internal and external issues.

Internal goals consist of overseeing and enforcing information management, privacy and security policies. Companies have strict internal requirements that include forming a board of directors, conducting initial director meetings, adopting bylaws, issuing stock to investors and recording any stock transfers.

Internal requirements mainly work to fight corruption or other corrupting elements a corporation may encounter.

Externally, there is a growing need to meet expectations of regulatory bodies, other authorities, shareholders, citizens, customers and employees alike. External compliance focuses on requirements imposed or enforced by a federal agency or state, while internal compliance addresses requirements that pertain to company operations.

Management of internal processes affects external compliance. This includes information governance, inventory, retention, disposition, security, vendor management and training.

Purpose of Evaluation

A program, practice, intervention or initiative is studied objectively to see how long the program has succeeded in achieving its objectives. An evaluation identifies what works well in a program or initiative and what can be improved.

The information collected as a result of an evaluation helps demonstrate the success of a program. The information gathered is of utmost importance for attracting and retaining current and potential investors' funding.

Things to Be Evaluated

Health-care compliance programs are essential to an organization's operation; they are the backbone of a workforce. However, compliance strategies for an organization need to be evaluated by regulatory bodies as part of their program evaluation process. Therefore, a department should implement methods for assessing compliance programs so that they can be run effectively.

Some of the methods that are used to assess compliance program effectiveness are:

1. **Reviews by an external independent firm**

An independent firm's review of compliance programs enables an organization to determine whether the program adequately covers the seven elements of an effective health-care compliance program and helps identify the strengths and weaknesses of the current program.

The seven essential components of a compliance program are:

- Standardized procedures and a code of conduct
- Compliance officers and a compliance committee

- Effective education and training
- Effective communication lines
- Auditing and monitoring of internal processes
- Discipline through well-publicized guidelines that enforce standards
- Response to detected offenses and remedial action.

2. **Annual compliance audits**

Audits of key elements of the health-care compliance program should be performed annually. The audit findings will indicate areas of strength and suggest areas for improvement. Annual audits should occur more frequently than a compliance program review, and compliance officers should create a remediation plan to eliminate weaknesses.

3. **Ongoing monitoring of processes and policies**

Monitoring activities is a must. Department/program managers need to participate in ongoing monitoring activities to identify potential fraud, waste and abuse issues. Annual audits will identify areas to monitor, such as high-risk areas like billing and coding and those identified by the OIG and government auditors.

4. **Surveys to measure compliance effectiveness**

Compliance effectiveness surveys can be appreciated as meaningful metrics when evaluating program effectiveness. Compliance officers conduct reviews, inspections, audits and monitoring activities related to compliance programs.

Implementation of Clinical Practice Guidelines (CPGs)

CPGs help advance clinical practice by establishing care standards supported by reliable scientific evidence, possibly reducing variability and improving clinical practice. Such guidelines seek to optimize patient outcomes, standardize care and facilitate shared decision-making among physicians, patients and caregivers.

Developing CPGs involves the following main elements:

- Defining the clinical problem
- Convening a multidisciplinary guideline development group
- Assembling a systematic review team
- Critically appraising the document after new studies have been conducted and updating it when new studies are conducted

- Implementing the plan into clinical practice; this final phase must identify barriers to implementation and formulation of effective dissemination strategies.

Service Quality

Providers of quality service must strive to provide patients with services that exceed their expectations. Good service influences patients' satisfaction and loyalty. Defining service quality is challenging because it is a unique and abstract concept with many meanings. Customers' attitudes toward the services they receive are described as their preferences or opinions.

Quality in health care consists of technical and functional elements. The technical aspect involves the skills, accuracy of diagnosis and procedures, whereas the functional aspect refers to what a patient gets from health care.

Monitoring is vital for gathering information about service quality and performance that cannot be gleaned from more traditional performance appraisal methods. It is important to conduct surveys and solicit patient feedback to know where the health-care system needs improvement.

Documentation

All health-care professionals must maintain records of medical documentation. This documentation includes information regarding patients' care, such as diagnoses and treatment. Comprehensive note-keeping in a hospital is essential for reporting hospital service activity and monitoring performance. The Joint Commission focuses heavily on patient safety and quality improvements to overall care.

Practitioner Performance

The primary objective of staff performance evaluations is to make employees aware of the quality of their performance, identify performance gaps and provide opportunities for future professional growth.

Employee performance appraisals involve two primary components: preparing a written appraisal based on employees' performance and reviewing employees' appraisals to receive and provide feedback.

The performance review should have a standardized format and be reviewed by one member of the organization. Reviews for new employees should be conducted on the ninetieth day or six-month mark to ensure that the arrangements between the employees and organization still feel right and that all responsibilities have been clearly defined.

Gaps in Patients' Experience

Patients' satisfaction with health-care services is crucial as a determining factor of quality. The philosophy of patient-centered care states that quality of service defines patient satisfaction. Service quality is defined as conformation to a patient's expectations.

Patients' views and expectations are measured in various ways. The Service Quality (SERVQUAL) scale developed by Parasuraman et al. continues to be the most widely used tool to measure patients' experience. The scale measures the level of patient satisfaction between a patient's perceptions and expectations.

Reportable Events for Accreditation

According to the Joint Commission, a sentinel event is an incident that results in death, permanent harm or severe, temporary harm to a patient. It is not primarily related to a patient's illness or underlying condition.

The Joint Commission strongly encourages but does not require reports of any patient safety event that meets the definition of a sentinel event. However, the Joint Commission's hospital accreditation regulations oblige accredited organizations to acquire internal instruments to collect and manage safety data on near-misses, hazardous conditions and sentinel events. Moreover, Det Norske Veritas (DNV) requires accredited organizations to report any adverse events.

How to Evaluate Them

A quality evaluation must be based on a clear concept of what it means to provide medical care. The evaluation process is also used to determine whether care is being provided according to set goals and whether the people who receive care appreciate the care quality. This evaluation can help determine ways to improve those services in the future.

In quality improvement research, monitoring and evaluating quality improvement initiatives occur at an applied research level. Research findings are intended to be used to inform policy and practice. Listed below are some ways to evaluate qualitative research.

Surveys

A survey is an excellent way to gather information that does not show up on lab results or come up in conversation with patients. Surveys can provide feedback through both private and anonymous channels, revealing what is happening in an organization and showing the organization how health facility characteristics affect health-seeker behavior and health outcomes.

Peer reviews

A peer review is a quality control measure for medical research carried out by professionals who critique each other's work to ensure its relevance, accuracy and significance. The peer-review code stipulates that reviewers must be honest, constructive and polite in their comments.

Focus groups

A focus group consists of individuals who discuss a particular subject, sharing their opinions and ideas. Focus groups operate based on interactions between group members and their moderator.

The purpose of a focus group is to collect preliminary data for interviews or surveys. This data can help users determine which issues they find important and determine how needs might be prioritized.

Complaints

Patients' complaints are a valuable resource to be monitored and improved for patient safety. Health-care organizations can identify systematic problems in health care by analyzing data stemming from negative patient experiences.

Complaint department employees have the responsibility of accepting complaints, collecting data and then passing the complaints on to colleagues, who have the authority to pass judgment.

Medication use

Medication Utilization Analysis (MUE) is a systematic method used to evaluate and improve how medications are used. A hospital must develop a safe and effective medication management system as part of a structured or mandated multidisciplinary program. The Joint Commission stresses the importance of developing such a system.

Chapter 10: Education and Communication of Issues

Accrediting and Regulatory Bodies

Accreditation is a formal verification offered by accrediting bodies that focuses on continuous improvement strategies and quality standards to ensure public safety. An accrediting body has no legal power to pass regulations. It is the process by which the authoritative body recognizes that an organization is competent to carry out the tasks.

The crucial accreditor in the United States is the Joint Commission. The Joint Commission's goal is to improve health care for the public by evaluating health-care organizations and motivating them to excel in providing safety and care of the highest quality.

The regulatory body is the authoritative body; it can be a government or public agency. A regulatory body enforces standards of competence that health-care professionals have to register, meet and practice. The regulatory body investigates complaints and checks the quality of education and training courses.

Designing Effective Quality Training Programs

Training programs have been used to teach quality improvement to health-care professionals for a long time. The continuous improvements to these programs are often focused on ways to provide experiential learning. Studies have shown that clinically focused quality improvement can improve patient safety and care. Healthcare QI training programs are aimed at preparing medical residents to enforce quality improvement and patient safety.

Planning is the first step toward quality improvement, and you need to analyze the problems and the best possible solutions. A quality improvement plan is a long-term commitment plan for a specific change. The plan defines what an organization wants to improve, how it will be improved, the anticipated outcomes and evidence of success.

A quality improvement plan should include:

- More than one QI method
- A built-in structure to keep the plan dynamic
- An attentive staff that listens and understands the needs of the stakeholders
- Steps and measures that are aligned with quality assurance
- Specified data that suits the organizations' goals

- Information collected from patients
- Clearly defined goals and aims.

Another helpful approach is the Six Sigma method, which is a data-driven framework that eliminates waste. The organization or team uses the DMAIC model (define, measure, analyze, improve and control) to define the problem, review historical experiences, analyze results and decide the best solution.

What is the quality improvement process?

In life-and-death situations, health care becomes the priority for quality improvement. Health-care quality improvement goals can be either functional or operational, allowing for creating process and outcome measures.

Most of the models and methodologies used for quality improvement contain four common steps: Plan-Do-Study-Act. First, you must identify the problem, then implement the change. Once the change has occurred, you must analyze the results. If the change was successful, you should act, meaning implement it on a broader scale.

STEEP is a quality improvement method developed in 1999 by the Institute of Medicine. Six goals have to be met to ensure patients' care and safety. These six goals are:

Safety: Avoid injuries to patients.

Timeliness: Reduce waiting time and try to mitigate the risk of any harmful delays.

Effectiveness: Provide services to all who could benefit from them, but refrain from providing services to those unlikely to do so.

Efficiency: Be productive and avoid wasting time.

Equitability: Provide care that does not vary in quality because of personal characteristics, such as gender, ethnicity and socioeconomic status.

Patient-centeredness: Handle patients with care and respect, and remain open to patient preferences, needs and values.

Education on Quality Improvement (QI)

Continuous quality improvement (QI) requires consistent improvement in education, especially in higher and public education. QI courses can be provided to professionals through the education system. QI courses were designed to merge theory and application. Their purpose is to improve an individual's knowledge and skills in the science of quality improvement. These individuals can be trained through QI courses to take action in a clinical setting that improves their patients' quality of care.

The development of QI education started in the late 1990s with professionals from different regions of the world, all speaking different languages. This proved to be a significant hurdle for developers. Thus, in collaboration with QI program developers, researchers at the Chalmers University of Technology began a two-year QI training program for health-care professionals in 2004. In total, 331 health-care professionals went through educational activities offering QI courses over 14 years. After the course, evaluations were conducted. They showed exemplary results: participants perceived the course as useful.

Concept map methodology

A concept map is a methodology that is designed to focus on the construct of interest. It combines qualitative and quantitative data collection and analysis through the process of brainstorming and multidimensional scaling. It helps an individual interpret results, which provides a visual representation of thoughts and ideas.

Cultural Change

Culture guides motivation and engagement and supports a company's overall strategy and plan toward success. Hospitals need to create a culture of safety for their patients in order to prevent errors and improve the quality of care. There are three objectives your health-care organization should take into consideration if it wishes to achieve great success. These objectives are:

A clear strategy

The health-care organization should develop a clear strategy that is easy for everyone to understand. Everyone should know and understand their responsibilities and how their actions might impact the patients or the entire organization.

Good leadership

Leadership is a social process that involves influencing people. You determine a direction, influence a group and direct the group toward a specific goal or mission. Changing or improving the organizational culture requires a good leadership team and consistency, focus and accountability.

<u>Effective communication</u>

Planning a set of goals and tools for an organization to bring change is very helpful. The team members must communicate with each other, and the leader should clearly define roles and responsibilities. Successful leaders should know how to communicate and deliver a consistent message. Leaders should make sure the employees feel valued and foster the confidence that they contribute to the betterment of the health-care organization.

Project Management in Health Care

Project management aims to predict as many errors as possible and plan, organize and control business activities. Health-care project managers focus on many projects, such as securing medical supplies, improving operations and planning emergency response rates. They identify problems and suggest possible solutions.

Some methods and techniques are used to complete projects in health care. They involve four stages:

<u>Initiate</u>: Know the scope of the project, its costs, results and possible errors. All of these are reviewed later by the management team.

<u>Plan</u>: Plan each step of the project, set the time, create the budget and assign tasks to meet deadlines.

<u>Execute and monitor</u>: Begin executing the steps as written in the plan. You must monitor and measure the progress regularly. This stage is intensive. Stakeholders have to sign off on every step of the process in the plan.

<u>Conclude</u>: End the project by creating a document that summarizes all outcomes.

Meeting Management

Meeting management is the process of meeting, planning and getting effective results for a health organization. In these meetings, the clinical team gathers to discuss patient reports, problems, uncertainties and solutions.

Meetings are valued very highly by health-care organizations because they are an efficient and effective means of communication. The challenge is to ensure that the meetings are focused, inclusive and productive.

In critical times, for example, if there is an increase in the number of patients, but the hospital lacks operating rooms, then a meeting is held to solve the problem. The team members discuss the problem and offer input. One person presides over the whole meeting. This person collates all the input and decides on a course of action.

Managing meetings is an essential skill for health workers to learn because it helps them make better decisions regarding their patients' treatment.

Effectiveness of Training Programs

There is a correlation between training programs and organizational effectiveness. Training evaluations help researchers understand and obtain relevant information on the impact of training programs. They specifically help researchers gather information about how trainees have demonstrated an improvement in their level of efficiency.

The major objective of conducting an evaluation is to develop an understanding of whether a training program has achieved its objectives or not. A good training program can improve people's effectiveness and increase their level of productivity.

Dr. Donald Kirkpatrick's model examines and evaluates the effectiveness of training programs. Developed in the 1950s, it is the best-known model for analyzing the effects of training programs at four levels, which are:

Reaction: Measuring trainees' reaction toward their training to understand the effects of the training program.

Learning: Measuring how trainees absorb information, knowledge and skills.

Behavior: Measuring how much trainees were influenced and the changes in their behavior.

Results: Measuring the impact of the training program and observing the results.

Licensure

Licensure is the process by which a government agency permits individuals to engage in each profession by certifying that they have achieved the minimal degree of competency required to ensure the public's health and safety.

To be licensed, a professional must pass certain eligibility requirements and at least one assessment to be eligible for a license. Nongovernmental organizations do not offer licensure. Once the license is received, it cannot be granted to someone else.

Dissemination of Information Within the Organization

Information dissemination is the method by which facts or information are distributed to the public. Internal dissemination is the process by which projects or information are shared in an organization. Conversely, external dissemination is the process of sharing information with people outside an organization on a bigger scale (i.e., from an individual to entire teams).

Information dissemination has to be planned carefully while you keep in mind the target audience, the message you want to deliver and the communication strategies you want to follow. A well-designed dissemination strategy can be beneficial; it can facilitate transparency in an organization.

Components of dissemination

The components of dissemination facilitate the translation of your research on a broader scale. They help researchers evaluate and determine if their research is progressing at the rate they wanted. Some major components considered in dissemination are:

Research findings: What are you disseminating?

End users: Who are you disseminating it to?

Dissemination partners: Through which organizations can you reach your end-users?

Communication: How will you convey your dissemination?

Evaluation: How was your information used or not used?

Tools and templates: Document your plan and track the progress.

Chapter 11: Health Data Management

Over recent years, information and communication technology has made rapid progress. Medical data management and health-care delivery systems have changed significantly with the advancement of technology. They have become more efficient and effective.

Health data management revolves around analyzing health-care data and managing it for the health-care industry's many stakeholders. Data collection within the health-care sector is becoming increasingly digitized as the volume of collected data increases in quantity. This digitized data collection benefits health-care organizations, and ultimately, patients, because it makes the compilation and analysis of information quicker.

In addition to organizing medical data, health data management is responsible for data integration and analysis, which helps medical personnel provide better and more accurate care to patients and develop insights that improve medical outcomes.

Infonomics helps us understand the three components required for health-care systems to become more informative, effective and manageable. The theory consists of three Ms: measure, manage and monetize, the purposes of which are listed below.

Measuring Data

This is the measurement of a company's willingness to invest in data because it is an asset. How much information does the organization have, and how valuable is that information?

Health-care organizations are constantly generating data throughout the system as they conduct business and provide services. After the health-care organization is aware of its data's true value, that asset must be managed by putting in place the programs, software and people required for its protection.

Managing Data

After a health organization has acknowledged its data's value, the next step is identifying where it comes from and how it is stored (managing data). Data management for health-care organizations means learning where the data is and understanding how to get that information into a form that can be managed.

Health-care organizations must have an adequate data operating system to take data under centralized control and ensure its availability across the organization.

Monetizing Data

Managing and maintaining data enables an organization to monetize it. How does the organization use its data?

A hospital's staff knows in advance how many beds are available for different patients (measure), where the beds are at a particular moment in time (manage) and how much they can charge patients staying in specific rooms (monetize). Data monetization involves more than making money. It can improve patient outcomes, lower health-care costs, discover new revenue streams, improve care providers' lives and optimize services.

Maintaining Confidentiality of Records and Reports

Confidentiality in health care is the commitment of medical practitioners to not reveal details of any patients' medical treatment. This essentially means that any information provided by patients to doctors and administration members who handle sensitive information must not be passed on to third parties, whether intentionally or not. Employees of medical centers are usually expected to maintain patient confidentiality.

A breach of confidentiality is an ethical and legal issue. There are various rules and regulations that prevent such breaches from happening, for example:

- Employees in health care are subject to confidentiality clauses in their contracts.
- Common law exists to maintain professional confidentiality.
- There is a requirement of the Data Protection Act that requires organizations to keep patients' personal and medical records safe.
- To be registered, an individual must abide by medical council guidance, which includes obligations relating to patient confidentiality.

Patients should always be informed about the information being collected about them, for what reasons and with whom it will be shared. Patients' privacy should be protected at all costs. It is imperative to inform patients and remind them that they can withhold consent.

However, confidentiality is not an absolute principle. There are important circumstances under which it is permissible to disclose a patient's medical records to a third party.

Disclosure without patient consent

Disclosure of information without a patient's consent is permissible under two instances: if it is required by law or when it is in the public interest. These instances are applicable if the patient cannot give consent or has explicitly refused to give consent.

An explanation for releasing information to the public usually revolves around the threat of serious harm to others. It can include any information relevant to preventing or detecting disease, offenses or prosecuting those who have committed them (whether voluntarily or involuntarily).

Disclosure with patient consent

Acquiring a patient's consent is the first, most obvious step to take when sharing information. Information about patients is frequently requested by insurance companies, employers or people involved with authority. Any information being disclosed should be done with the patient's permission and consent. If consent is not given, then the information should not be shared.

A doctor should always ask for a patient's consent before sharing information, as it demonstrates respect toward the patient and is an essential part of good communication between both parties.

Ways to protect patient confidentiality

With the development of computerized medical records and the coalition of health-care systems, people have become increasingly concerned about potential threats to patient confidentiality. It is essential to protect and safeguard patients' confidentiality, which can be done in the following ways.

Develop sound policies and confidential agreements

It is important to design agreements and policies that cover all aspects of confidentiality. A confidentiality agreement, in essence, is a legally binding document that states what information is confidential and cannot be shared with third parties. Everyone at an organization must agree and abide by the agreement, understand it and sign it. They should share it with their patients to demonstrate that their organization upholds its strict procedures and protocols.

Provide regular training

When people fully understand the reasons behind the policies and practices, they are more likely to adhere to them. It is important to hold regular training sessions for all doctors, nurses, administrators and staff members to remind them how important the confidentiality rule is and provide them with a refresher on staff duties and expectations.

Store all data on secure systems

Patient data sets have increased exponentially as the standard of health care improves, the population increases and technology becomes more sophisticated. This can make it challenging to accurately store information, both in terms of creating a safe place to store large amounts of data and making this information easily accessible.

To keep patient data safe, it is imperative to use the highest security and digital protection standards. Access to this data must be controlled to ensure only the necessary personnel have access. Security passwords that control access can also be utilized to prevent information leaks.

Designing Data Collection Plans

Data collection includes gathering, analyzing and interpreting different kinds of data from multiple sources. Gathering quality evidence is the basis of data collection as it seeks to answer all the posed questions. With the help of data collection plans, an organization can deduce quality information. Data collection is essential for improving the quality of information. It also helps personnel glean insights into medical problems.

Sampling Methodology

Imagine that you have a large organization with substantial numbers of people. Most businesses or organizations do not have enough time to connect with consumers individually. In many cases, it is impractical to try to reach every person on a list. To solve this problem, you must use a sampling methodology.

A sample is, in theory, a subset of a population that represents an accurate reflection of the population. This is a tricky task, as populations can be diverse. There are five main accepted methods of sampling:

Random sampling

A random sample will eliminate biases that can affect the validity of a study. You need to choose and select the desired sample size from a population so that each observation has an equal chance of being included in the study until the desired sample size is achieved.

Systematic sampling

To achieve regularity in sampling, systematic sampling can be used. It establishes a set of rules that must be followed. Systematic sampling is more convenient than random sampling. It also assures an equal probability of inclusion in the sample for each sample unit.

Convenience sampling

Collecting samples by convenient means is a collection strategy in which samples are taken in convenient locations for the sampler.

Clustered sampling

When populations naturally group themselves into clusters, cluster sampling is used. In this case, researchers use subgroups instead of individuals. Cluster sampling is more efficient than other methods because some work is already done: a group is already defined.

Stratified sampling

The stratified sampling method is a way of taking samples from populations divided into subpopulations. Clustered and stratified sampling methods might seem similar. Still, the significant difference between both is that in stratified sampling, the samples are collected at random, and only certain clusters are used.

Tools and Techniques

A data collection tool is a device/instrument used to collect information, such as a paper interview form or computer-assisted interviewing software. Data collection can capture useful evidence used to facilitate analysis, leading to the formulation of convincing and credible answers to the questions posed. It is important to decide which data collection method should be used as different approaches suit different purposes.

Quantitative and Qualitative Methods

Data collection is divided into two types:

Quantitative

Data is measured in the form of numbers (e.g., percentages, comparisons).

Qualitative

This type of data is in nonnumerical form. It describes observed qualities or characteristics shown by something or someone and is usually written in narrative form (e.g., observations, descriptions).

Several of the methods covered here are quantitative, dealing with something that can be counted. Others are qualitative, which means that there are factors other than numbers to be considered. Records, questionnaires and documents are quantitative. Interviews, observations and oral histories are qualitative.

Primary data collection in organizations can be carried out using several methods. These methods include traditional and simple approaches to data collection and analysis, such as face-to-face interviews and more advanced approaches, such as data mining.

Qualitative Data Collection Methods

Qualitative data collection looks at the information in greater detail and lends a greater understanding to raw data. This method evaluates psychological factors, such as patients' thoughts and feelings.

Listed below are the three most used qualitative data collection methods:

- Ethnography
- Grounded theory
- Phenomenology.

Ethnography

Anthropology defines ethnography as the study of human societies and cultures. It helps researchers understand how people live their lives. A subject's viewpoint is taken rather than that of the researchers. Researchers use observation to discover the reasons why patients behave the way they do. Ethnography is a useful qualitative approach to address a particular type of research question.

Grounded theory

Grounded theory has been an influential force in the acceptance of qualitative methods in various social science applications. This theory is used to explore social interactions within human society. Various methods are used to explore these interactions, such as:

- **Participant observation:** Researchers study subjects by immersing themselves in the subjects' lives and interactions.

- **Interviews:** The purpose of interviews is to gather data on various topics from the subjects. The interviews can be formal or informal.
- **Document or artifact collection:** Data must be examined to interpret documents, elicit meaning, develop meaningful insights and gain empirical knowledge. Materials used by a group can provide researchers with valuable information about the people within a group.

Phenomenology

The study of phenomenology discusses people's experiences with some events or encounters. Reactions to unusual occurrences are measured using this method, so it is important to think about the whole picture, not just facts and figures.

One example of phenomenological research is analyzing the traumatic experience of people involved in natural disasters.

Quantitative data collection methods

Quantitative observation is more accurate than qualitative observation because a numerical measurement is used. Researchers can evaluate qualitative data through numerical analysis, which is essential for quantitative research.

There are three primary quantitative research methods:

Descriptive: Based on observational data collection, descriptive research describes the current status of a variable. It is a statistical analysis of a population sample using an approach to collect quantifiable information.

Correlational research: Correlational research is a way to assess the relationship between two quantitative variables by evaluating how strong their correlation is. The relationship between two variables can be positive or negative, where the strongest correlation between variables carries the magnitude (+/-) 1.

Experimental research: Experimentation, also known as true experimentation, employs the scientific method to gather information regarding cause-and-effect relationships in the environment. This method makes sure that all factors that potentially influence the phenomenon of interest are controlled. Research participants in an experiment are divided randomly between a control group and a treatment group.

Data Collection Tools

Interviews

Interviews have open-ended questions. No matter how the questions are asked, they are more customized and responsive than other primary data collection methods.

Questionnaires and surveys

There are many ways to analyze survey and questionnaire data, and you can assign numerical values to the data to speed up the analysis. This is particularly useful if you are trying to get vast amounts of statistical data from a large number of people.

Observations

During an observation, researchers gather information without asking questions. This method derives more subjective data, as observers' bias can inevitably leak into the data.

Documents and records

Research that utilizes existing data from documents and records can yield valuable data.

Oral histories

Oral history refers to the narration of personal experiences, opinions and past facts, as told by participants.

Collection and Validation of Data

Validation of data is a decision-making process resulting in either a valid or invalid set of data. General rules express the acceptable combinations of values that a decision-maker must use. Rules are applied to data. If data satisfies the rules, then data is deemed valid for the final use.

Data must be gathered (collection) and then verified (validation) before being input. Managing or processing input data includes storing, classifying, updating and calculating input data.

Identification of External Data Sources for Comparisons

External data refers to any data information captured, processed and disseminated via sources outside a company. External sources of finance are sources outside the business. There are four relevant external data types:

1. **Open data:** The data is freely available; it can be published without restrictions.
2. **Paid data:** The data is available commercially; this data is offered in exchange for money.
3. **Shared data:** This type of data is shared between organizations.
4. **Social media data:** Users of social media share this type of data.

Development of Scorecards and Dashboards

Health-care organizations need performance management tools like dashboards and scorecards that are interactive, enabling them to measure and manage performance effectively. An organization's performance is monitored through both dashboards and scorecards. These help an organization run smoothly and efficiently.

Scorecards are best suited to managing strategy, while dashboards are more suited to managing operations.

Dashboards

Large sets of information can be visualized with a dashboard, a business intelligence tool used primarily by companies. Companies can evaluate their operational performance in real time since data is constantly being updated.

Scorecards

An organizational scorecard is a tool that outlines an organization's objectives concerning strategy. Those tools are useful for firms that need to make better strategic decisions based on performance measurements relative to their objectives.

Selection of Measures

A selection of measures should be made to address health priorities, such as issues related to health conditions. This measure addresses areas in which improvements in quality of care could impact the actual and potential levels of a patient's health.

When considering possible health-care quality data measures, three major categories of criteria should be considered: importance, scientific soundness and feasibility.

Importance: Measuring what is important

- Health implication: What are the direct and indirect health effects of this problem?
- Meaning: Are consumers and policy makers interested in this area?

- Susceptibility to be influenced by the health-care system: Can the health-care system handle the problem?

Scientific soundness: Measuring the validity of the measurement

- Measure validity: Does it capture what it is supposed to?
- Reliability: Does the measurement provide consistent results?
- The explicitness of the evidence base: Are there any tests available to back the measurement?

Feasibility: Measuring the practicality of the measurement

- Existence of prototypes: Has the measure been used before?
- Measurement of cost: How much will it cost to collect the data?
- Access to required data: Can data be collected to the extent required?

The Importance of Health Data Management

Compared to the traditional method of managing health records by storing paper records, now there is an excess of medical records that have become difficult to maintain. Data management has reduced this problem by storing and organizing data in a digitized form.

The health data management system enables an organization to analyze medical data to make patient care more efficient and produce insights that can facilitate better health-care outcomes while safeguarding the data's confidentiality and security.

Chapter 12: Health Data Measurement and Analysis

In health data measurement, the model for improvement emphasizes the importance of measurements in improvement efforts. Hundreds of health-care organizations in many countries have successfully used this tool to transform the way they provide care to their patients and improve health and quality outcomes.

Health analysis refers to collecting and analyzing data so that the health-care organization can use it for decision-making. Among the other data sets included in health care, analytics are medical costs, patient behavior and pharmaceuticals. Health-care analytics can be beneficial on both macro and micro levels. They can affect operational efficiencies, improve patient care and reduce overall costs.

In health-care management departments, health-care data analysis provides a combination of financial and administrative data and information that can help improve patient care and services. With the help of health data measurement and analysis, providers can:

- Deliver quality care using data-driven methods
- Optimize scheduling and staffing processes to minimize patient wait times
- Streamline processes related to making appointments, processing insurance and providing referrals to improve patient satisfaction and quality of care
- Upgrade patient experience by improving treatment in a more personalized fashion
- Use population health data combined with information about a patient's health to identify at-risk patients.

Using data management systems

Data management aims to enable people and organizations to optimize the use of data while collecting, storing, retaining and utilizing it in the most secure, efficient and cost-effective manner within the limits of policy and regulations. There are many ways the health-care industry compiles information, such as:

- Physician notes
- Appointment scheduling
- Billing
- Insurance claims
- Electronic health records
- Health surveys

- Test results
- Prescriptions.

Organizations have started to rely on intangible assets to create value, making a robust data management strategy increasingly important. An organization's management of digital data involves a range of policies, procedures and practices. The task of data management covers a wide range of factors, such as:

- Creating, accessing and updating data across multiple data tiers
- Using cloud storage and on-premises storage
- Managing disaster recovery and high availability
- Learning about new apps, analytics and algorithms across the web using data
- Making sure data is kept secure and private
- Maintaining data retention schedules and compliance requirements while archiving and destroying data.

A data management platform enables large companies to easily collect and analyze tiers of data by utilizing existing or new tools developed by a software vendor or a third party.

Using Tools to Display Data and Its Evaluation

Displaying or visualizing data is the process of using graphics to present information, statistics, and data. Chart, graph and map displays offer a quick and clear way of reading and understanding the information or statistics. Display tools and technologies are important for analyzing massive amounts of information.

Heath data includes different forms of information. The type of data produced within the health system depends on the patient's experience, hospital response, treatment or therapy. However, sometimes data can be specific to a disease, such as collecting data regarding the COVID-19 outbreak.

Tools for visualizing health data

Medical and public health organizations are increasingly integrating health data visualization because of the increased use of available tools. Decision-makers can examine metrics or scan trends more rapidly with a set of interactive reports. Health-care organizations can use several types of dashboards for different purposes.

1. Operational dashboards: These provide real-time results of what is occurring in a hospital setting. For example, they may show admission details that can be reviewed throughout the day.

2. Strategic dashboards: These show patterns and trends over time. For instance, executives at a hospital can see how patient lengths of stay have changed over the course of several months.
3. Analytical dashboards: These can provide data on a broader scale. One example of using an analytical dashboard is analyzing a large collection of patient medical records to find specific trends.

Presenting data in interesting ways can be accomplished through several visualization approaches. The kind of information being presented differs from visualization designs to the audience to whom it is being presented. Some common visualization tools are:

- Charts
- Tables
- Graphs
- Maps
- Infographics
- Dashboards.

Various evaluation techniques are used to determine a program's success, effectiveness and efficiency by gathering information throughout its implementation. Health-care organizations can develop a plan to help clarify an evaluation approach and give it direction.

The assessment process should include questions, measures, approaches to assessing and processes for collecting data. An evaluation can be an excellent means of communicating information so that the community can influence policy decisions and promote a sense of accountability.

Quality management

In today's data-driven world, quality management relies on several statistical tools for monitoring and controlling quality. Data collection, analysis and root cause identification are used as quality tools for problem-solving, process improvement and performance measurement.

Pareto chart

Bar graphs and line graphs can be combined to create a Pareto chart. This chart can help identify the facts necessary for setting priorities. It also organizes and presents information in a way that is easy to comprehend.

A Pareto chart can help an organization:

- Invest in the most critical areas
- Prioritize the likely causes of a problem
- Help the critical few stand out from the uncritical many.

Run chart

By tracking data over time, trends or patterns can be observed. A run chart is a line graph that shows data points as they change over time. It is a simple and effective tool to help determine if changes are effective or not. The data may show:

- Variances
- Trends (performance improving, remaining constant, or deteriorating).

To measure improvement, a team should use a balanced set of measures in this analysis. They can use a run chart to visualize data over time for these measures because it is the most practical and effective way of seeing whether changes are making improvements or not.

Control chart

A control chart visualizes process performance and shows whether or not it is within acceptable limits. Control charts can be used to track the project's performance figures, such as cost or schedule variance, along with many other metrics. Such charts can also be used to:

- Confirm that the process remains stable
- Monitor any conditions that require the team to react
- Look for any patterns in the run of results.

Scatter-plot diagrams

Scatter-plot diagrams are used to evaluate the correlation between two variables. A scatter-plot diagram displays two pairs of numerical data, with one variable on each axis to examine relationships between the variables. These diagrams can show:

- The validity of the cause-and-effect relationship
- What causes poor performance
- How independent variables affect dependent variables.

Using statistics to describe data

As a branch of applied mathematics, statistics involve data collection, description, analysis and inference from quantitative data. The two main branches of statistics include descriptive statistics, which describes samples and populations' properties, and inferential statistics, which uses these properties to test hypotheses and draw conclusions.

A descriptive statistic describes a study's data's characteristics by providing simple summaries about the sample or measures. These foundations are used in every quantitative technique of data analysis, alongside simple graphics analysis. You can find out what the data shows rather than analyzing it directly through descriptive statistics.

With the help of inferential statistics, statisticians can draw conclusions about a population by examining a sample's characteristics. They can also calculate the reliability of applying these conclusions to a population. Statisticians can calculate the probability of statistical significance from the sample size and distribution of the sample data.

Mean: This is a mathematical average calculated by dividing a set of values by the total number of values in a data set. It is used to estimate a population from one data set derived from a sample of the population.

Standard deviation: The standard deviation of a data set is the value that represents the deviation from its mean and is calculated as the reciprocal of the variance of the data set. Each data point is calculated as the square root of variance by measuring its deviation relative to the mean.

Correlation: Correlation is a statistic that is used to show how two different types of variables are linearly related. It is a useful tool for describing a subject's position without saying what caused the event in the first place.

T-test: Inferential statistics, such as the t-test, is used to determine if there is a significant difference between two groups' mean averages, which may have certain common characteristics. A t-test is used to test an assumption made about a population with the help of hypothesis testing.

A computer program can be used to speed up large sample t-test calculations. The t-test is one of the most used statistics in studies of an inferential nature.

Using Statistical Process Control

Statistical process control (SPC) is a statistical method for measuring, monitoring and controlling processes. SPC is considered a tool to establish quality control. It is the scientific visual method used to monitor and control processes by eliminating processes that vary in a particular way.

Statistical

Statistics is a branch of knowledge about gathering, summarizing, analyzing and inferencing information from data.

Process

Process uses a combination of machinery and people to respond to input resources and turn them into the desired output (goods or services).

Control

Control involves a system, policy and procedure put in place to deliver the overall target.

An organization must constantly strive to improve quality, efficiency and cost control. Through SPC, companies can make a shift away from detection-based quality control toward prevention-based quality control. With the help of SPC graphs, organizations can better predict how a process will behave.

Common and special cause variation

We can never obtain identical results for two different situations, no matter how hard we try. Every piece of data will show some variation. Variation is defined as "the number given to each member of a group to indicate how widely they differ."

According to Walter A. Shewhart and W. Edwards Deming, natural patterns can be used to classify all possible causes. The common causes of variance include quantifiable, expected, common, historical, random and nonroutine causes of variance. The common causes of variance show where the process can go when the special causes of variance are eliminated.

The particular cause of variance differs from the common cause of variance because it takes into account factors with known effects on the process. A special cause of variance consists of nonquantifiable, unanticipated variances, typically unrecognized in the product manufacturing process. There are usually special cases determined by a change of input parameters or a sudden change in conditions.

Adjustments to the processes, components or methods can usually eliminate special causes of variance. They may cause problems if they are not eliminated.

Random variation

Random variation conforms to the laws of probability, acting statistically like the chance function of the universe. An estimation of the magnitude of a parameter, based upon the average of a sample of measurements of a treatment effect, is prone to deviation from that parameter's true value. As the sample size grows, the number of errors shrinks. But as the differences between estimates shrinks, precision increases.

Trend analysis

Trend analysis is a statistical method used to examine past trends and predict future movements based on those trends. Researchers can use this method to predict future behavior based on old market data and to collect information about past market behavior and plot the data on a horizontal line to gain meaningful information.

Data analyzers measure and explain trends and patterns in big, noisy data over time. A trend could be positive or negative in a data set over time.

Interpretation of Data

As digital communication has become more prevalent, data is being generated at a greater rate, which requires increased interpretation and analysis. Data interpretation involves reviewing data through predefined processes and inferring significant conclusions from the data that are based on the relationships studied.

Information collection and interpretation allow an organization to make the best-informed decisions possible by acquiring useful and usable information. Many organizations and individuals benefit from data collection and interpretation.

It is important to break down complex data into simpler terms for the general public, which is what analysts do when they analyze raw data. This analysis can be done through two main methods: qualitative and quantitative.

Qualitative data interpretation method

The qualitative data interpretation method is used to analyze and understand qualitative data, which is also known as categorical data. With this method, instead of using numbers or patterns to describe data, the text is used. Qualitative research consists of gathering data directly from the people who are being researched. This data can be harder to analyze than quantitative data.

Nominal and ordinal qualitative data are the two main types of qualitative data. An ordinal data set is usually labeled with numbers, and coding is not required at the time of data collection. In comparison, a nominal data set requires coding before the data can be interpreted appropriately.

Quantitative data interpretation method

Quantitative data models are usually used to analyze numerical data. In these models, the collected data are listed in numerical form.

Quantitative data is divided into two major categories: discrete and continuous data. Continuous data types further include interval data and ratio data, all of which are numeric. Analyzing quantitative data involves mathematical models such as standard deviation, mean, median and range.

- Mean: A mean is a number representing the average derived by dividing the sum of the values by the number of values found in a data set.
- Standard deviation: Standard deviation measures the degree to which the responses align with or deviate from the mean. This provides insight into the data sets by describing the degree to which they are consistent with one another.
- Frequency distribution: Frequency distribution is used to assess the demographics of the respondents or the frequency at which respondents provide a particular response.

Comparison of Data Sources

A consumer's health record is a primary source of data in health care. In health care, data can come from patient laboratory tests and procedures. When data taken from the health record is used for database and registry purposes, it is called secondary data.

Researchers often rely on two kinds of data sources to conduct their studies: primary and secondary.

A primary source is an original record, usually an eyewitness account, from the time the subject is being researched. Primary sources can take many forms, including newspapers, journals, court documents, church records and census records. A primary source of data is one in which the researchers directly collect the information for their research purpose or a specific research project.

Surveys, administrative records, medical records, vital records, surveillance, databases of chronic diseases and peer reviews are the most common places to find health statistics.

Administrative data

As organizations deliver and pay for care, they generate administrative data on the characteristics of those they serve, their use and utilization of services and how much is charged for those services. Information from claims, encounters and enrollment is used to develop the report.

A report is:

- Accessible electronically
- More economical than acquiring medical record data
- Accessible to a broad population of patients and across insurers
- Written in accordance with uniform codes and practices.

Participation in External Reporting

External reporting requires organizations to produce well-documented reports that can be distributed to individuals and the public. These reports do not include information that is considered confidential unless it is critical to achieving the organization's objectives.

Core measures

A core measure is a nationally standardized system designed to improve patient care. The process provides the most appropriate treatment at the right time to patients.

Patients at risk for blood clots can receive preventive medications, while stroke victims can receive rehabilitation provided they have earned a grade equivalent to that of a grade I patient.

Providing quality health care through core measure processes reduces complications and leads to better patient outcomes.

Patient safety indicators (PSIs)

Patients safety indicators (PSIs) are measurement tools that provide insights into potentially avoidable safety events that present opportunities for improving health-care delivery. In hospital settings, they focus specifically on problems and events that can happen after surgeries, procedures and childbirth.

PSIs can be used to identify issues in hospitals that ought to be studied further and help assess the frequency of adverse events and complications within hospitals. Health-care researchers use PSIs to gather information regarding adverse events and identify possible areas of improvement.

HEDIS bundled payments

The National Committee for Quality Assurance (NCQA) introduced the HEDIS (Healthcare Effectiveness Data and Information Set) scoring system to measure health plans' clinical quality performance.

Health plans influence the clinical care of their members through activities and programs delivered by providers. They also collect and analyze data on the care members receive.

The bundling arrangement allows for multiple providers' payment collectively for handling services provided within a single, pre-described episode of care. In HEDIS, a bundled payment model is where providers and/or health-care facilities receive an overall payment for all services rendered to a patient during a specific period.

Bundled payments are likely to benefit multiple health-care system stakeholders by shifting financial concerns from the payer to the provider and shifting accountability and responsibility.

Chapter 13: How to Identify Opportunities for Improvement

Providing quality care means keeping the health-care system safe, effective, patient-centered, efficient, timely and equitable. Health-care quality is defined by the Health Foundation as a multidimensional standard of excellence.

According to the Health Foundation, several approaches are necessary to deliver sustained health-care quality improvements. Professional requirements, government initiatives and economic drivers are some of the factors that influence workplace behaviors.

Organizations can use various methods and models to deliver sustainable health care to their patients. Organizations can develop and monitor their plans by engaging their employees, establishing clear objectives and deploying a systematic change approach.

Discussion About Opportunities Available

It is essential to understand improvement opportunities in the health-care system by setting goals. This should be done in a top-down manner, where the overall medical organization goals are defined in a pyramid structure. Determine how to analyze the departments, the processes and the organization's goals using dashboards and data sampling.

The following tips can help improve the health care offered by an organization.

Analyze data and outcomes

Before an organization can improve its health care, it is necessary to identify improvement opportunities first, then establish baseline outcomes. After that, electronic health records must be analyzed, along with outcomes studies and other sources to determine areas that require improvement.

Set goals

Based on the above findings, organizations can then establish concrete objectives to improve performance in the most critical areas. Precise and quantitative measures are necessary to implement the needed changes. Improvement goals should be based on the following six pillars of quality health care:

Safe: Make sure patients are not injured while getting the care they need.

Effective: Optimize care; do not overuse ineffective care or underuse needed care.

Patient-centered: Honor individuals and respect their choices.

Timely: Reduce waiting time for patients and caregivers.

Efficient: Cut down on time wastage.

Equitable: Reduce health disparities among ethnic minority groups.

Build a well-balanced team

According to the IHI, one of the primary steps in the improvement process is forming a balanced team. Team members with varied backgrounds and skills are the best choice for creating an effective team. A team should include a senior leader with oversight responsibilities and advocacy responsibilities, an expert clinical decision-maker and a team leader who can manage the day-to-day tasks and keep the team on track.

Develop an actionable improvement plan

A team must develop an actionable improvement plan to achieve their goals both efficiently and on time. This plan should include specific measures, protocols for achieving those measurements and specific goals, all of which require a thorough analysis of an organization's database.

Establishing Priorities

The task of setting priorities for a health-care organization or a single patient or service is defined as determining the importance that should be assigned to each service, service development or patient at a given time. Health-care resources are insufficient for patients at many times. Therefore, prioritization of resources is required to achieve sustainable health-care improvements.

Priority-setting criteria

Strategic fit

This is the extent to which clinical services advance an organization's strategic objective. The candidate must "fit" into the organization's values, vision and goals. Based on this criterion, strategic planning should focus on establishing long-term objectives rather than short-term political concerns.

Academic commitments

These commitments emphasize the importance of clinical education in teaching, recruiting, training and retaining medical professionals. Academic health science centers are lauded for their research role, which can result in the invention of new best practice standards, new medical knowledge and technological innovation.

Community need

Community-based health services recount patients' needs and requirements within the organization's local catchment area. This recount can include the demand for health care in the area, both current and future trends in population size and the patients' use of health-care facilities.

Clinical impact

Medical staff must always have sufficient clinical competence to provide safe and expert care to patients. Therefore, clinical impact is defined mainly in terms of the service volumes needed to ensure safe and effective care. Additional factors relevant to clinical impact could be:

a) The health service provided in the local area is unique
b) Measures taken to prevent diseases are effective
c) The service is of high quality.

Development of Action Plans

Action planning is a method organizations use to determine their needs, set clear goals and develop strategies to achieve them. Health organizations need to make an action plan if they wish to bring changes to ensure that information, products and services are understandable and accessible.

The purpose of an action plan is to follow a cycle of planning, practicing and reviewing to achieve change and self-renewal. An action plan can be used to address new learning needs or to translate the skills and knowledge learned through a formal training program into an everyday job.

Implementation of Performance Improvement Methods

Performance improvement initiatives are routinely carried out within health-care organizations to improve clinical outcomes, enhance patient experiences and reduce operating costs.

If an organization wants to improve performance, it must have multifunctional and multidisciplinary teams that are fully aware of the process and are enthusiastic about participating. Communication must happen at all steps of the improvement process. Therefore, communication between the leadership and team members should be the top priority when implementing changes in an organization.

In health-care systems around the world, three industrially based methodologies have been successful in achieving dramatic results. They are:

Lean

Lean is a set of operating philosophies and methods that emphasizes a continuous improvement process by using a set of instruments and rules. These rules and instruments eliminate time wastage, improve medical service quality and increase patients' safety and comfort.

This methodology enables health-care providers to respond immediately to patient needs and focus on healing them by securing what they need when they need it. Lean organizations start by defining value from the customer's perspective. Then they aim to consistently improve the flow of value to each customer.

PDCA (Plan-Do-Check-Act)

PDCA (Plan-Do-Check-Act) was first proposed by Walter Shewhart in 1929 and was popularized by W. Edwards Deming in the 1950s as a learning model. The PDCA cyclical structure allows for continuous improvement. It provides a framework for solving problems, implementing policy and improving processes.

The planning phase includes an assessment of the current procedure or another procedure. At this stage, it is essential to understand the yields. The next stage is used to evaluate the information and results gathered during the do stage. In the act stage, document changes are made, and others are informed about them.

Six Sigma

The health-care sector has for many years almost exclusively used Six Sigma as a management tool to enhance patient safety and quality. The Six Sigma concept can be defined as a process that is expected to provide 99.99966 percent of production opportunities without defects.

With Six Sigma, an organization aims to increase its process outputs by identifying and removing errors and mitigating variability in the processes. Six Sigma follows the DMAIC process, which is:

Define

Identify the problems, opportunities for improvement, project objectives and customer requirements.

Measure

Measure the efficiency of the process.

Analyze

Understand root causes for variation and poor performance (defects).

Improve

Get rid of root causes and improve performance.

Control

Take action to exert control over future process performance and improvement.

Identifying Champions

An employee who is dedicated to improving a particular area of the company is known as a champion. In health-care settings, champions play a key role in improving the organization.

Effective champions must be able to identify gaps and inefficiencies in the organization's way of doing things, be confident in their ideas and speak out. Their goal must be to ensure that the highest-quality care is delivered and that no substandard care occurs.

Health-care organizations tend to designate champion roles to team members and expect them to be responsible for specific aspects of care. A champion must value high-quality care and facilitate the change required to improve both internal and external quality of care within the health-care system. Service quality, employee retention and employee motivation can all be improved by appointing a health-care champion.

Chapter 14: How to Implement the Steps

Implementation is the action taken to carry out a plan, a method, a particular measure or procedure. Health-care workers need to take proper measurements in order to implement quality improvements in their organization.

A systematic approach is essential to implementing innovations, new procedures, protocols and best practices. A variety of recommendations—usually related to professional performance and health-care delivery—are included in proposals for change.

An effective way to tackle these problems is by focusing mainly on the problems where change will contribute to improved patient outcomes and not the ones with little to no change.

The achievements of health initiatives depend on the performance of the implementation processes. Though many approaches to implementing a program or steps may appear straightforward at first, careful planning in advance, multiple stakeholder involvement and addressing unique contexts all require complex processes.

Establishment of Teams and Their Roles

Health-care delivery is best executed within an effective team environment. Teams with effective performance are needed due to the increasing incidence of comorbidities and the increasing complexity of medical specialization.

Health care has evolved in a way that calls for quality patient care. As a result, medical professionals have been focusing increasingly on teamwork. Sharing values and principles helps develop an outstanding team that can provide exceptional care to patients.

Nowadays, the concept of teamwork is accepted worldwide as crucial for constructing a more effective and patient-oriented health-care delivery system. To identify best practices for using team-based care in a systematic, scientific manner, researchers need to understand this system's core elements.

Providers in team-based health care work collaboratively with patients and their caregivers to deliver health services to individuals or groups of individuals. The goal is to achieve shared goals within and across settings to sustain coordinated, high-quality care for patients. A team approach that includes shared responsibilities and shared accountability has great benefits in health-care systems.

There are several types of health-care teams, such as:

Core teams

Core teams are responsible for the care of patients. A core team usually consists of team leaders, members who are direct care providers, such as nurses, dentists, pharmacists, assistants and case managers.

Coordinating teams

These teams provide both operational management as well as coordination of functions and resource management.

Contingency teams

A contingency team deals with an emergency or specific event. They are responsible for direct patient care during critical situations.

Ancillary teams

The mission of the ancillary team is to provide supporting activities to the core team. This team aims to create a safe, comfortable and secure environment within the health-care facility and improve efficiency and safety.

Support services

This group provides administrative, logistical and relational support for a health-care facility. It includes secretaries and the executive leadership of the health-care unit. A team of professionals continuously oversees the cohesive and efficient operation of the entire facility.

Several reasons have contributed to teamwork becoming an important health intervention. For example, medical care is becoming more complex and specialized, so medical staff are forced to offer complex health services while learning new methods.

Teamwork lowers the number of medical errors by up to 40 percent and increases patient safety. It decreases issues that culminate in burnout. Research shows that physicians are more likely to be involved in patient care if their staff is working together with them. Nowadays, the responsibility of a patient's care is given to an entire team of health workers who coordinate their efforts in order to afford their patients better care than ever before.

Usage of Quality Tools and Techniques

More than 40 years ago, Avedis Donabedian proposed that health-care quality could be gauged by assessing its structure, processes and outcomes. These structures could include health insurance, hospitals' bed capacity and advanced training of nurses.

A few factors can influence health care, including mortality, patient satisfaction, improved health status, environmental factors and behavioral factors.

The total quality management model (TQM) involving process-oriented, team-based and decision-making processes, as well as transformational change, seeks to create an environment for continuous process improvement. In this approach, the organization is committed to quality and improvement from the top down.

The research attempts to assess problems that produce generalizable results, whereas quality improvement projects and strategies try to address quality issues and make a positive difference. Listed below are some models that have been used to bring sweeping changes across organizations.

Plan-Do-Study-Act (PDSA)

Health-care improvement projects and studies using the Plan-Do-Study-Act method can lead to favorable outcomes by making positive changes in health-care processes. The PDSA method has been widely used to improve continuous service. One of its unique features is that it focuses more on assessing small changes rather than significant changes, as that is more effective to execute.

Root Cause Analysis (RCA)

RCA, a technique often employed in engineering and similar to critical incident analysis, identifies the underlying causes of an event and understands its potential repercussions. When human error is suspected, RCA can be used to identify trends and assess risk. RCA is further discussed later in this book.

Fishbone Diagram

Ishikawa diagrams, which are sometimes known as "fishbone diagrams," are graphic plots used to explore possible causes of an effect. Team members use a fishbone diagram to better understand the possible underlying causes of the quality-of-care problem and focus efforts on these possible causes. Quality improvement can be modeled in many different stages but is mostly used in root cause analysis. There are many benefits of the fishbone diagram, such as:

- Understanding that a cause or a combination of causes can help teams achieve the desired outcome
- Illustrating the relationships of the causes to the effects and helping to identify their relationships
- Facilitating the identification of areas that need improvement.

Failure Modes and Effects Analysis

Health Care Failure Mode and Effect Analysis (HFMEA) is designed to recognize potential failures and their causes before future treatment is delivered. Through the HFMEA process, opportunities for improvement in current services are provided.

HFMEA is a process used to identify the contributing factors and effects that eventually lead to failures in a process or practice. It is a process used to systematically assess the potential failure points of current services. It also determines the relative impacts of different failure modes and elements in a process.

HFMEA is particularly useful for determining the process elements that require the most change. It improves patient safety and efficiency by identifying issues early and resolving them before they become a problem.

The provision of health care must occur within a complex system that relies on the coordinated actions of doctors, nurses and patients. Five steps are used to implement HFMEA. They are:

Define the topic

According to the purpose of the research, a topic may be selected that is a response to a sentinel event or a near miss. Other tools, such as environmental and safety walkthroughs, error reports and even customer complaints, reveal analytical opportunities.

Assemble a functional team

Team members must be committed to identifying potential improvements and working on the project as a whole. They must also receive sufficient time and resources to make the project successful. Leadership support and buy-in are essential to a successful HFMEA. Leaders must recognize the value of the process and should support the changes the team implements.

Describe the process

The team needs to prepare a detailed chart of the process so that they fully understand all the steps involved. This understanding is achieved by creating process maps that illustrate the sequence of expected events in the process. A process map represents complex processes hierarchically and includes attributes such as cycle time and delays between phases, responsible persons, cost at each step and wastage.

Conduct the HFMEA

In this process, a team needs to identify each of the subprocesses causing potential failure, then understand the different failure modes resulting from each subprocess. Any mishap during the completion of a process step constitutes a failure. The team should evaluate the potential effects of each failure, particularly the impact on patients, but also the impact on the department's operation. If the failure occurs right before the patient intervention, more harm is likely to occur to the patient.

Determine actions and outcome measures

The process failures should be identified, and strategies must be put into place to prevent future occurrences. A proper implementation plan should include (a) defined outcome metrics and timelines, along with specific corrective actions, and (b) the person who will implement the plan, educate staff and monitor results.

Process Mapping

A process map visually represents the entire project and gives insight into the systems and processes that enhance the implementation of health-care quality improvement projects.

Communicating the essential details and sequence of a project to team members through process mapping is more effective than detailing processes in documents.

Optimizing patient pathways involves the use of coordinated, multidisciplinary practices to optimize efficiency and efficacy by removing ineffective and unnecessary care. Using process mapping data as a resource, we can redesign the clinical pathway to improve the overall quality and efficiency of patient care while focusing primarily on activities that benefit patients.

Monitoring of Project Deadlines

The management function's basic elements are planning, organizing, staffing, leading and monitoring a project. A leader's ability to balance leadership and teamwork with a need to focus on people is the key to success in project management. A project manager needs to keep a sharp eye out for where the project is heading, with glances at the dashboard at the right times.

Defining the scope of a project's deliverables and priorities is important to successful fixed-deadline project planning. All functional leads should work together to create a meeting plan for information gathering. Reverse planning makes sure that scope, time and expected quality are maintained.

When you plan by working backward, you begin at the end and come up with a plan of action. Reverse planning provides a map of what needs to be accomplished and makes it easier to stay on track.

Scope statement

Defining the scope of a project's deliverables and priorities is important to successful fixed-deadline project planning. All functional leads should work together to create a meeting plan for information gathering. Project deliverables need to have criteria and a clear list of deliverables.

The outcome of a project must be determined before it commences. Deliverables that cannot be accomplished before the end of the project should be excluded. The parameters of the project must be analyzed. It is advisable to assess the risks in less time so that contingency costs and time can be appropriately allocated.

Work breakdown structure (WBS)

WBS is needed to make decentralizing decisions possible. WBS must facilitate appointing people in charge of direct tasks so decisions can be made with ease. In addition to organizing the project team, WBS helps coordinate the implementation of change across departments.

A team leader breaks down the WBS by task and specifies the requirements for each task that has to be achieved. Leaders also identify the quality standards that management favors, as well as approximating the start and end dates of each task.

Activity list

There are detailed activities required to complete each work package mentioned in the WBS. Each activity and its predecessors are listed. The activity is evaluated, the risks assigned to opposite cases are listed and possible responses for generating more activities are also noted.

Activity sequencing

Activities are expressed logically, with graphs demonstrating the connections between each activity. The most popular is the precedence diagram method(PDM). This graph illustrates things in a clear, linked manner. Nodes signify activities, and arrows imply the internal relationship between them. By using this graph, a team can identify the milestones and the necessary end date for achieving them, assign the people in charge and determine possible responses to the risks.

Resource estimating

In this step, the performance of resources (people, equipment and material) is determined to predict the point when they will be required. A list of activities and a complete inventory of all the resources, their characteristics and their availability are necessary. A hierarchical approach is used for gathering activity resources. The risks of resource availability are analyzed, and the time reserves for responding to them are also determined.

Activity duration

Resource capacity needed to perform the assigned tasks is used for estimating the duration of the activity. Probabilities of achievement of the estimated duration are examined, together with duration reserve.

Reverse planning

This planning method uses the critical path method, which is based on a nonlinear process. Early start, early finish, late start and late finish times are expressed as time remaining before the completion of the project by a fixed deadline.

Strategy to optimize critical path

The following strategies should be applied if, after performing reverse planning, the project starting date is shifted ahead: (a) fast-tracking, which determines if one or more sequential activities can be performed in a parallel manner by analyzing the critical path in this way; (b) crashing, in which, for each critical activity, the shortened duration is analyzed in terms of the cost associated with shortened duration.

Schedule

Once we have optimized the critical path and have set a start and end date, can a schedule be developed? The schedule should be structured according to the WBS: deliverables, work packages and activities.

Micromanagement and risk management

The critical activities of the project should be micromanaged. All critical activities must be clearly outlined and continuously monitored to ensure that they are understood by the people who have to execute them. Actions for prevention and corrections should be designed by supervisors and/or team leaders to support the project manager who makes the decisions.

To reduce risk, all the initial risks should be consolidated with associated risks to the work package, the schedule, the critical path optimization strategy and all the previously identified risks.

Evaluation of team effectiveness

Team training has been identified as the best strategy for improving patient outcomes and an effective method for improving team effectiveness. Teamwork reduces hospitalization time and costs, decreases unplanned admissions, improves accessibility for patients and coordinates care more effectively.

Patients can receive many benefits from an effective team, such as enhanced satisfaction, acceptance of care and improved health outcomes. Team benefits include increased efficiency using health-care services, enhanced communication and professional diversity.

Team effectiveness assessment identifies general issues within the team. Once the assessment is complete, the focus can shift to enhancing important skills. Teams are assessed through a questionnaire based on eight dimensions:

- Purpose and goals
- Underlying team relationships
- Problem-solving ability
- Roles
- Team process
- Intergroup relationships
- Passion and commitment
- Skills and learning.

Moreover, groups may review the results and make recommendations for team development. Individuals may compare their opinion of the team to the views of others.

Evaluation of the Success of Performance Improvement Methods

Health-care organizations can improve their performance level and achieve success if they adhere to a few principles, such as the three elements of the Triple Aim: patient experience, health and cost. If these factors are kept constant, a continuous improvement initiative can become successful. You can combine a qualitative and a quantitative measure of the initiative's value to determine the measure of success in such an initiative.

Success can be measured in a continuous improvement initiative, acting as a check in the Plan-Do-Check-Act cycle. If the reported results do not meet the quality standards, adjustments will be made, and the cycle will be repeated. There are three ways of assessing success:

- Financial results
- An assessment tool
- The views the stakeholders hold.

Documentation of the Results Obtained

Documentation of the results of any analysis is necessary so that a reviewer can recreate the analysis. Technical documentation serves as a written record of the functionality of a particular process. Good documentation inspires confidence and makes it feasible for future enhancements to be implemented. If an organization has guidelines for preparing a document, they should always be followed.

The organization can request a general rating of employees' performance, specific ratings of specific aspects of their performance or a combination of ratings with qualitative information. Observations, comments and examples will prove more helpful to the individuals in the team than a numeric rating.

Observations about team members' performance should be recorded in a document in as much detail as possible, and conclusions should be backed up with hard evidence.

Chapter 15: Assessment of Patient Safety

Hospitals are required by law to establish patient safety standards to provide a safe environment. These initiatives help hospitals build patient safety capacity, improve patient care safety and involve patients in improving health-care safety.

Patients' safety is assessed through patient safety-friendly hospital assessment programs, either before initiating a patient safety program or as part of an ongoing program. These programs provide institutions with a means to determine patient safety levels. They also enable organizations to analyze, assess and improve patient safety levels to implement a patient safety program or as part of a regular program.

A comprehensive assessment of patient safety benefits hospitals in several ways. It signals commitment and accountability to the public about patient safety. The tool offers valuable benchmarking information, shows areas of weakness and motivates staff to improve patient safety.

Definition of Patient Safety

According to the WHO, "Patient safety is the absence of preventable harm to a patient during the process of health care and reduction of risk of unnecessary harm associated with health care to an acceptable minimum."

The concept of patient safety emerged in the wake of the increasing complexity of what it means to provide health care and the rise in patient harm.

According to the American Medical Association, the concept of patient safety in the health-care system refers to "the pursuit of methods to reduce the risk of medical errors as well as utilizing best practices for treating patients."

Health services across the world should be effective, safe and people-centered. These services must be the focus of quality essential health services.

Importance of Patient Safety

Safety protocols can lead to fewer medical mistakes and may prevent adverse patient outcomes. The health-care system is committed to ensuring patient safety; it is the cornerstone of high-quality health care.

Health-care workers and technology work together to ensure successful the treatment of any patient. This is the result of a chain of factors instead of a single individual. Health-care professionals can prevent illness, injury and infection by ensuring a safe environment for patients.

Patient safety also plays a key role in reducing costs related to patient harm and improving health-care systems' efficiency. The provision of safe services can restore people's trust in health-care systems.

A quality framework establishes the foundation for quality improvement across the organization. It is designed to make sure the organization delivers value to patients and people.

Role of Technology in Ensuring Patient Safety

Meeting patients' global health-care needs presents a series of challenges for clinicians and medical staff, from protecting patient information and supporting an aging population to managing staffing shortages.

More than 250,000 deaths in the United States per year are said to result from medical errors. According to a recent Johns Hopkins study, medical errors are the third-leading cause of death after heart disease and cancer. Hence it is important to find a solution to this problem. Technology can help immensely.

Technology plays an important role in doctor-patient communication, medical safety, reduction of potential medical errors and improvements in patient experience. Patients can easily access their health information through technology, thereby increasing their engagement as consumers. This empowers them to participate more actively in decision-making and gives them more information about their health problems.

Electronic Health Record (EHR)

It can be time consuming and difficult for health-care professionals to maintain patients' medical records on paper. Consumers want access to their health-related data and information without having to go to their health-care provider's office; therefore, digital solutions are essential.

Electronic health records are a paperless, patient-centered electronic version of chart notes. They keep information up to date and accessible only to authorized users. This technology allows health data to be shared with health-care providers across multiple organizations and is managed in a digital format.

Physician productivity and patient satisfaction are key areas where EHR systems can improve medical practices.

Physician productivity

Health-care organizations are now implementing EHRs to speed up physician diagnosis and digitize administrative tasks.

Patient satisfaction

EHRs give patients the ability to track their health data and medical records to understand where their health needs to be improved.

Abduction Security Systems

Infant protection is a major concern for caregivers, parents and law enforcement officials. With an appropriate system in place, it is easier to lower the likelihood of harm coming to infants by caring for newborns in a facility where they cannot be separated from their mothers. This policy also lowers the chances of a mismatch occurring between baby and mother.

Nurses can contribute to infants' safety and security by following prevention plans established by the Joint Commission, an organization that develops security standards and conducts assessments to identify abduction risk within hospitals. In addition to installing an infant security system, the facility should also become a test site for mother-free identification bands, which offer an additional security layer.

Real-time protection

New infant protection technologies work with WiFi networks to inform staff and patients of a baby's location and well-being in real time. Mobile devices, such as smartphones and nurse call systems, are also used to manage medical records.

Experts agree that the core concept of tags and alerts remains the same; however, how they are utilized in hospitals and computer software has changed. New tags feature smaller batteries and longer battery life, so they are more convenient.

Stand-alone products

The most widely used solutions for preventing child abduction are readily available on the market as stand-alone products. Greater security can be afforded through stand-alone systems; there is also less risk of data theft or hacking incidents.

Hospital security systems have to interface with infant protection solutions, such as fire alarms for door lockdown and elevator lockout controls if needed. With integrated video surveillance in its safety and security systems, a hospital can monitor patients once an alarm is activated.

Smart pumps

Smart infusion pumps have recently been introduced to the health-care industry. These devices enable patients to receive medication directly into their veins. This smart technology prevents patients from receiving dangerous over- or under-doses that could cause harm or even death.

Once activated, the device is configured to the needs of a particular space, such as the intensive care unit (ICU). Once the clinician selects the drug and concentration from the list, the device will then administer the medication.

Smart pumps come with the ability to log all alerts. These alerts allow the hospital to pinpoint any programming errors or near misses that were averted.

Alerts

In case of an emergency, health-care institutions and medical centers have a responsibility to ensure employees', patients' and visitors' safety. It is crucial that information be disseminated in a timely and reliable manner during an emergency. Communication within a facility is vital, whether this is to employees only or the entire building, without making patients anxious and exceeding building noise standards.

Providing alerts and alarms to care team members directly through their mobile devices can improve patient safety in many clinical scenarios.

Participation in Risk Management Assessment Activities

The concept of risk management is one of the most effective management tools for ensuring overall health and safety (and others' well-being). However, many people do not realize that risk assessments are a legal requirement for employers and self-employed people.

The definition of a risk assessment is a systematic process of finding hazards, assessing them and managing them within the workplace. Employees (and others) can eliminate, reduce or control risks to their health, safety and well-being by conducting a risk assessment.

Developing and implementing risk management programs for health-care providers is based on thorough research and study. Research results may sometimes contradict presumptions made in risk management practices, so risk managers need to keep current with relevant information their organization offers.

Risk management plans should cover patient-specific risks and be well documented; all patients should be able to read them.

Employees and physicians can reduce patient risks by conducting standardized tests for their employees, providing counseling services for personnel working with patients and ensuring that training procedures are followed accurately.

To eliminate or control any health risks, it is necessary to complete an appropriate risk assessment before performing a particular activity or task.

Chapter 16: Implementation of Patient Safety Programs

In health-care organizations, strategic planning focuses mainly on developing and implementing patient safety strategies so patients are safe and receive better services.

The best way to improve patient safety is to cultivate a safety culture in health-care organizations. A safety culture can be defined as a coordinated behavior, including individual and organizational behavior, rooted in shared beliefs and values, to minimize harm in treating patients.

A successful safety and health program will improve employee morale and productivity by equipping employees with the training necessary to work in a safe environment.

Purpose of Patient Safety Programs

A growing body of medical knowledge has contributed to the evolution of patient safety as health care becomes more complex. Health-care provision aims to avoid and reduce errors, risks and harm to patients.

The Patient Safety Program aims to minimize patient risk while improving safety, reducing the incidence of medical errors and preventing them from occurring. There are a few core features that every patient safety program must include. These core features are as follows:

Safety is a key value

Employees need to engage in patient safety initiatives through an organization committed to patient safety as a core value.

The top leads the way in safety

A hospital leader's active involvement in patient safety is also vital to patient safety programs.

Safety alerts are reported

To ensure patient safety and prevent errors, hospital leaders must identify gaps in patient safety and mistakes that occur.

Transparency is integral to the safety

An effective patient safety program will promote transparency, shared learning and trust.

Safety incidents are disclosed

Patient safety and health programs exist to prevent injuries, illnesses and deaths and remove the financial hardship and suffering that these events can cause for patients and their families.

Evaluation of safety activities

Evaluating campaigns, services, programs or government initiatives allows organizations to assess how they systematically achieve the objectives. Evaluations help management determine which strategies accomplish objectives both efficiently and effectively.

It is essential to evaluate improvement programs in health care to determine whether interventions work. The following health-care aspects can be assessed:

- Health-care effectiveness – The benefit available to people by improving their health
- Efficiency – A comparison of the outputs or effects to the cost
- Acceptability – The social and psychological acceptance of health-care practices involving people
- Health equity – Equitable distribution of health-care resources among individuals or groups

Assessment may be performed prospectively or retrospectively. Evaluation carried out prospectively is a more robust approach to data collection, resulting in a more fruitful topic and more likelihood of obtaining satisfactory results. The process of prospective evaluation can be built into the implementation or maintenance of a service or project.

Usage of Safety Principles

Organizations that provide health care are required to establish safety systems to prevent harm to patients, their families and friends, medical professionals, contract-service workers, volunteers and other individuals engaged in the practice of medicine.

Safety is a quality metric. The following are its core principles:

The patient is first

Providing safe, accessible, timely and high-quality care is a priority across the continuum of care through a partnership between patients, families and caregivers.

Safety is paramount

Achieving effective, efficient and positive outcomes for patients and staff involves identifying and controlling risks.

Self-responsibility

The policy meets the needs of patients, health-care staff and the general population globally. The employee job description sets out specific responsibilities and accountabilities.

Determined authority

A manager directs subordinates to carry out their responsibilities.

Clearly defined accountability

The system permits a single individual to handle the responsibility on behalf of groups, functions or committees.

Leaders are expected to lead

A safety culture can be created in clinical and social care by motivating people toward a common goal and bringing about structural change.

Multidisciplinary work

Individuals and groups have a mutual dependency in delivering services, so interdisciplinary work must emphasize interdependence. Positive collaboration is therefore essential.

Performance support

This involves supporting performance in an ongoing process, considering professional autonomy and clinical professionalism in a business environment and contributing to individuals' and organizations' capabilities and knowledge through the management of services and employees.

Culture of openness

A culture of openness entails a culture of trust, honesty, respect and care, where achievements are recognized for their value and patients have open access to information about safety and adverse events.

Constant quality improvement

A learning environment and system demonstrate a commitment to the advancement of service delivery with the confidence to deliver quality, not just controlling processes.

The safety principles define the guiding principles for safety measures and related regulations that aim to protect people and the environment against the effects of radiation and the safety of infrastructure and activities that present those risks. It is essential to adapt these principles to provide a safe and secure environment.

Systems Thinking

Systems thinking is a problem-solving method that stresses the interaction between the various elements surrounding a problem and the elements affected by the problem to achieve the system's goal. Systems thinking has been used by many firms in fields ranging from health care to agriculture.

The term *systems-based practice* is used in health care as well. Essentially, a system-based practice's fundamental premise is seeing a patient's treatment within the overall health-care system. Effective implementation of systems-based practices improves patient outcomes and safety. A systems approach is often applied at the system level to reduce waiting for lines in hospitals, ensure better screening practices to detect diseases earlier and improve public health.

High Reliability

A reliable organization creates systems that enable it to achieve its goals with minimal errors and to avoid potentially catastrophic mistakes. The principles of reliability have been used effectively in the manufacturing industry, such as improving the rate at which systems consistently produce the appropriate outcomes—to improve safety and process reliability.

Reliability principles are an essential component to improving health-care systems by eliminating defects in care processes, increasing patient outcomes and consistency in care delivery and reducing costs.

Health-care systems at these hospitals apply a three-step model for implementing reliability principles:

- Stop malfunctioning operations or systems.
- Identify and mitigate failures.
- Identify critical failures and redesign the process accordingly.

Human Factors Engineering

In human factors engineering, the aim is to design systems that maximize safety and minimize errors in complex environments while always considering that people are fallible.

Human-machine interfaces are developed through an HFE process (user-centered design). This design process focuses on user characteristics and end-user testing; it takes user requirements, characteristics and preferences into consideration.

Health-care organizations are increasingly in need of human factors and systems engineering expertise. The relationship between employee and patient safety is explored, for example, by understanding the effects of work systems and physical ergonomics. This knowledge will prove valuable for health-care organizations when it comes to employee health management.

Health-care organizations can improve quality and safety by integrating human factors expertise and systems engineering expertise across various health-care organizations.

Health-care organizations face numerous barriers to the widespread distribution of this knowledge, including the need to understand applying human factors and systems engineering in health care, not considering the importance of systems design in various aspects of health care and using technical jargon and terminology.

Participation in Safety Management Activities

The safety management framework consists of the principles, framework, processes and tools that may be applied to help prevent accidents, injuries and other risks in an organization.

The participation of workers and their representatives is essential, as any safety and health program is effective if it succeeds. Worker participation refers to all workers and the establishment and evaluation of the safety and health program.

Root Cause Analysis (RCA)

The goal of root cause analysis (RCA) is to locate problems by identifying their causes and finding appropriate solutions. RCA shows clear benefits in preventing and solving problems from their roots rather than just addressing symptoms and putting out fires.

Primarily, the purpose of RCA is to identify an event's root cause. A second goal of the process is to understand how to fix entirely, compensate or learn from any root causes within the system. A third objective would be to systematically prevent current challenges or repeat successes by using the knowledge gathered from this analysis.

A process modeled on diagnostics is used to find both primary causes and contributing factors in RCA to prevent a problem's recurrence.

Failure Mode and Effects Analysis

Failure modes and effects analysis (FMEA) is a systematic, proactive approach that assesses a process to identify potential failure points and the relative consequences of those failures to identify the most worthwhile parts to change. During FMEA, the following items are reviewed:

- Various stages of the process
- Fault modes (How could something go wrong?)
- Failure causes (What caused the failure?)
- Failure effects (How does each failure affect our goal?)

Teams use FMEA to evaluate possible incidents and prevent them by taking proactive measures to avoid adverse events rather than waiting after problems occur. This focus on prevention can reduce the chances of harm to patients and staff. A risk-based FMEA approach is particularly beneficial in assessing the impact of a proposed change on an existing process and assessing a new process before implementation.

Review of Unexpected Events

Investigating adverse events can provide information on incidents and show where interventions would be most effective. Assessing the progression of adverse events over time helps organizations determine whether improvements are occurring. Additionally, data relating to adverse events may reflect patient safety concerns at either an organization or a local level.

In the United States, the global trigger tool (GTT) was developed to assist chart reviews in identifying adverse events that would otherwise require many hours of analysis. The

GTT enables teams to rapidly analyze patient notes to evaluate triggers that can signal harm from the patient's perspective.

Review of Incident Reports

This process completes auditing, investigating, classifying, analyzing, responding to and reporting the incident management process's functions. The review process ensures that all pertinent information is documented in the report. Whenever an incident occurs, it is best to describe who, what, when, where, how and why it took place.

The incident report should include a comprehensive picture of the actions taken following a productive review process, feedback and recommendations. A senior or independent person should review an incident report in conjunction with the employee who informed the senior.

Test 1

Organizational Leadership Questions

(1)   What is a current law passed by the state or federal government called?

(A)   Contractual obligation

(B)   Political obligation

(C)   Statutory obligation

(D)   Moral obligation

(2)   Implementing which of the following methodologies can streamline health-care processes?

(A)   Qualitative and quantitative research

(B)   Advancement of technology and implementation of technology

(C)   Scientific and social research

(D)   Practice management system, patient engagement and care coordination software

(3)   Who is responsible for designing and promoting strategic planning in health-care organizations?

(A)   Unit leader

(B)   Government

(C)   Doctors

(D)   Pharmacists

(4)   Internal best practices in an organization are promoted by?

(A)   The owner of the organization

(B)   People working in the organization

(C)   Government agencies

(D)   Consumers

(5)   Providing better health care means improving:

(A)   Doctors' and nurses' experiences

(B)   Facilities in the organization

(C)   Safety, effectiveness and efficiency

(D)   Research in health care

(6)   Lewin's change management model was created by:

(A)   Kurt Lewin

(B)   James Watson

(C)   William Lewin Kurt

(D)   Alan Guth

(7)   What compliance must a health-care organization adhere to in order to ensure patient privacy?

(A)   System and Organization Controls (SOC)

(B)   Sarbanes-Oxley Act (SOX)

(C)   International Organization of Standardization (ISO)

(D)   Health Insurance Portability and Accountability Act (HIPAA)

(8)   What is the purpose of health promotion programs?

(A)   Promoting healthy behavior that reduces diseases and deaths

(B)   Evaluating health-care workers

(C)   Teaching health-care workers

(D)   Analyzing a health-care system

(9)   What is the first step of Lewin's change management model?

(A)   Refreeze

(B)   Analysis

(C)   Change

(D)   Unfreeze

(10)   The Patient Protection and Affordable Care Act (PPACA) serves as a/an:

(A)   Framework for the organization for data collection

(B)   Evaluation of protection provided to patients

(C)   Framework for employers to stay updated with needed health-care reforms

(D)   Analysis of the services provided by health workers

(11)   What are regulations?

(A)   Laws fulfilled by an organization

(B)   Legal requirements provided through a procurator

(C)   Patients who take surveys

(D)   Laws enforced by employers

(12)   Nurses serve as a vital link between:

(A)   Patients and government

(B)   Patients and doctors

(C)   Patients and agencies

(D)   Patients and regulatory bodies

(13)   What is used to safeguard patient data while keeping track of it?

(A)   Electronic medical records

(B)   Record accounting documents

(C)   Recording journals

(D)   IT service management

(14)   Medicare compliance programs need participation from whom?

(A)   Patients

(B)   Federal agencies

(C)   Doctors and nurses

(D)   Organizations' employees

(15)   What are the three hard elements in the McKinsey 7-S Model?

(A)   Structure, skills and staff

(B)   Strategy, structure and systems

(C)   Strategy, skills and structure

(D)   Style, staff and skills

(16)   What is a change agent responsible for?

(A)   Evaluating an organization's health system

(B)   Putting theory into practice

(C)   Helping a project manager

(D)   Changing the rules of an organization

(17)   What are the four common steps that every quality improvement method consists of?

(A)   Plan, understand, evaluate and implement

(B)   Analyze, perform, evaluate and act

(C)   Plan, do, study and act

(D)   Analyze, evaluate, process and implement

(18)   What is medication utilization analysis (MUE)?

(A)   Prescribing medication to employees

(B)   Analyzing the type of medication a patient is taking

(C)   Determining the patient's medication

(D)   Systematically improving how medications are used

(19)   Who is obligated to follow OSHA standards?

(A)   Doctors and health workers

(B)   Employees and patients

(C)   Government and public health organizations

(D)   Public health organizations and patients

(20) What is the purpose of the nudge theory?

(A) It enables patients to give reviews about the health-care organization.

(B) It enables employees to perceive and understand the need for change.

(C) It enables health workers to evaluate the health-care system.

(D) It enables employees to take part in training programs.

(21) What is a sentinel event?

(A) An incident that results in death, permanent harm or severe temporary harm to a patient

(B) A traumatic event that traumatizes a patient and his or her family

(C) An event that causes harm to health workers

(D) An incident that threatens the life of patients' families' mental health

(22) What does certification demonstrate?

(A) Competence in learning about health care

(B) Commitment and dedication to the profession

(C) Evaluation of a training program

(D) Analysis by regulatory bodies

(23) What is the Kübler-Ross Change Curve?

(A) The implementation of changes in health care

(B) Emotional reactions rather than rational objections as a response to change

(C) Understanding the need for change through logical thinking

(D) Changing the way the health-care organization processes

(24)   How can a health-care organization effectively implement change when the workers experience emotional reactions rather than rational objections as a response to change?

(A)   Enforce the changes

(B)   Provide therapy for these workers

(C)   Empathize, understand and help the workers

(D)   Implement the changes with negotiations

(25)   How does a change management model help a health-care organization?

(A)   It helps facilities bring changes to the organization.

(B)   It provides assistance to the doctors and patients.

(C)   It prepares the organization to deal with resistance.

(D)   It helps develop a plan for implementation.

(26)   What are internal best practices?

(A)   Practices introduced by employees of the organization

(B)   Practices introduced by the patients of the organization

(C)   Practices introduced by the external part of the organization

(D)   Practices introduced for implementation by the government

(27) Who is responsible for the success of a health-care organization?

(A) The doctors

(B) The staff members

(C) The patients

(D) The government and agencies

(28) What is the most important nursing responsibility?

(A) Facilitating patient nutrition

(B) Providing care to patients and their families

(C) Monitoring patient health

(D) Assisting doctors

(29) What does the ADKAR change management model represent?

(A) Appreciation, desire, knowledge, abilities and reinforcement

(B) Awareness, desire, knowledge, ability and reinforcement

(C) Application, development, keys, ability and recognition

(D) Ability, development, keys, application and recognition

(30) What are the five stages of the Kübler-Ross Change Curve?

(A) Resistance, violence, weakness, inferiority and fear

(B) Anxiety, perplexed, confusion, fear and awkwardness

(C) Happiness, calmness, awkwardness, joy and admiration

(D) Denial, anger, bargaining, depression and acceptance

(31)   What is the goal of Det Norske Veritas Germanischer Lloyd (DNV GL)?

(A)   Help the patient's family and friends

(B)   Manage doctors and nurses

(C)   Safeguard life and give quality assurance

(D)   Perform evaluations for training programs

(32)   What is the functional aspect of quality in health care?

(A)   What the government gets from health care

(B)   What doctors get from patients

(C)   What patients get from health care

(D)   What employees receive from patients

(33)   What is the SERVQUAL scale developed by Parasuraman et al. used for?

(A)   To evaluate an organization's health-care system

(B)   To measure workers' competence

(C)   To measure patients' medical treatments

(D)   To measure patients' experience

(34)   What is the nation's highest presidential award for performance excellence?

(A)   The Bafta Award

(B)   The Booker Award

(C)   The Baldrige National Quality Award

(D)   The Pulitzer Award

(35)   What should employees do if they witness noncompliance, fraud, abuse or ethical or privacy issues?

(A)   Report it to the receptionist

(B)   Report it to the Medicare compliance department

(C)   Consult their peers

(D)   Report it to the accrediting body

(36)   What does VR and AR technology provide to health-care organizations?

(A)   Help understanding patients' needs

(B)   A multisensory experience to better understand patients' conditions

(C)   An evaluation of the patient's experience

(D)   A systematic analysis of the patient's thinking

(37)   What type of problem is the McKinsey 7-S Model ideal for identifying?

(A)   Problems in the patients

(B)   Problems in health workers

(C)   Problems within the organization

(D)   Problems within the doctor's treatment

(38)   What is the primary objective of staff performance evaluations?

(A)   Awareness of the treatment provided to patients

(B)   Awareness of employees' quality performance, gaps and ways to improve

(C)   Awareness of the organization's reputation

(D)   Awareness of doctors' quality performance

(39)   How is recognizing employees helpful?

(A)   There is a reduction of accidents by workers during patient treatment.

(B)   It improves the organization's facilities.

(C)   There is a reduction in patient complaints.

(D)   There is a reduction in staff turnover and an increase in productivity and positivity in workers.

(40)   What is Kirkpatrick's model used for?

(A)   Evaluating patient feedback

(B)   Analyzing the organization's health-care efforts

(C)   Evaluating and analyzing patient safety.

(D)   Analyzing and assessing the impact of training programs

Health Data Analytics Questions

(41)   Which of the following studies does health data management refer to?

(A)   Analyzing health-care data

(B)   Analyzing monetary data

(C)   Analyzing statistical data

(D)   Managing data privacy and security

(42)   What is health data management responsible for?

(A)   Provision of monetary information to patients

(B)   Organization of medical data

(C)   Improvement of communication and technology

(D)   Integration of statistical and medical data

(43)   Which of the following refers to the application of infonomics?

(A)   Understanding business requirements

(B)   Digitizing the health-care sector

(C)   Improving medical outcomes

(D)   Understanding the components required for health-care systems to become more effective

(44)   What are the three Ms of infonomics?

(A)   Measure, manage and monetize

(B)   Manage, monetize and meditate

(C)   Measure, monetize and mark

(D)   Measure, manage and make

(45)   What does measuring data refer to?

(A)   Measurement of patient data

(B)   Measurement of statistical data

(C)   Measurement of monetary data

(D)   Measurement of a company's willingness to invest in data

(46)   What is the data collected by health analysis used for?

(A)   Managing organizations' facts and figures

(B)   Managing monetary and statistical facts

(C)   Making decisions in health-care organizations

(D)   Improving low-quality medical outcomes

(47)   What can providers do with the help of health data measurement and analysis?

(A)   Deliver quality care using data-driven methods

(B)   Provide efficient and effective medical information

(C)   Improve organizations' policies and regulations

(D)   Provide monetary benefits to organizations' employees

(48)   What does data monetization involve?

(A)   Improvement of patient outcomes

(B)   Management of the company's assets

(C)   Management of health-care staff

(D)   Improvement of staff routines

(49)   What does confidentiality in health care refer to?

(A)   The breach of an ethical issue

(B)   Not protecting the patient's privacy

(C)   Disclosing patient's medical treatment information

(D)   Commitment of medical practitioners not to reveal patients' medical treatment details

(50)   What kind of issue is a breach of confidentiality?

(A)   Ethical

(B)   Moral

(C)   Spiritual

(D)   Ethnical

(51)   Under which of the following circumstances is it permissible to disclose patients' information without their consent?

(A)   If it is required by law or the public interest

(B)   If it is required for the company's benefit

(C)   If it is required for the employees' best interests

(D)   If it is required for monetary benefits

(52)   What ensures good communication between a doctor and a patient?

(A)   Maintaining patient confidentiality

(B)   Breaching of an ethical issue

(C)   Coming to reasonable monetary agreements

(D)   Disclosing a patient's medical records

(53)   Among the following, what is the major cause of exponential growth of patient data sets?

(A)   Improvement of health care

(B)   Decrease in population

(C)   Decline in medical advancements

(D)   Improvement in staff behavior

(54)   Imagine that you have a large organization with a large number of employees. Most businesses do not have enough time to connect with customers individually, including large groups, such as residents of large cities. In many instances, it is impractical to try to reach every person on such a list. What methodology can be used to solve this problem?

(A)   Classification

(B)   Sampling

(C)   Data standardization

(D)   Data visualization

(55)   On which levels can health-care analysis be beneficial?

(A)   Macro levels

(B)   Micro levels

(C)   Both A and B

(D)   None of the above

(56)   How can hospitals identify at-risk patients?

(A)   By using patients' experience

(B)   By delivering low-quality care

(C)   By optimizing and managing their patients' medical data

(D)   By using population health data combined with information about individual patients' health

(57)   What is the goal of data management?

(A)   To enable people to optimize the use of data

(B)   To enable people to use data-driven methods

(C)   To optimize the scheduling and staffing processes

(D)   To streamline processes related to making appointments, processing insurance, and providing referrals to improve patient satisfaction and quality of care

(58)   What is the basis of data collection?

(A)   To gather quality evidence

(B)   To enable the organization to grow financially

(C)   To ensure patients' health

(D)   To disclose patients' medical data

(59)   Which of the following is a characteristic of systematic sampling?

(A)   Each observation from the population has an equal chance of being included in the study.

(B)   It ensures an equal probability of inclusion in the sample for each sample unit.

(C)   Samples are taken in locations that are convenient for the sampler.

(D)   It is a way of taking samples from the population that can be divided into subpopulations.

(60)   What is a confidentiality agreement?

(A)   Agreement stating the disclosure of patient information

(B)   Agreement stating the breach of sound policies

(C)   Legally binding agreement stating what information is confidential

(D)   Agreement of a plan to protect company interests

(61)   What can be a possible explanation for releasing a patient's medical information to the public?

(A)   It can be used to regulate employees' routines.

(B)   It provides monetary benefits to the organization.

(C)   It revolves around the threat of serious harm to others.

(D)   It can be used to improve an organization's reputational resources.

(62)   Which of the following is characteristic of convenience sampling?

(A)   Each observation from the population has an equal chance of being included in the study.

(B)   It ensures an equal probability of inclusion in the sample for each sample unit.

(C)   Samples are taken in locations that are convenient for the sampler.

(D)   It is a way of taking samples from the population that can be divided into subpopulations.

(63)   Which of the following is true regarding the data collection tool?

(A)   It is a device used to collect information.

(B)   It is a device that allows populations to naturally group themselves into clusters.

(C)   It is a device that helps in taking samples from the populations that can be divided into subpopulations.

(D)   All of the above.

(64)   How many types is data collection divided into?

(A)   Two

(B)   Three

(C)   Four

(D)   Five

(65)   How can the policies related to confidentiality be maintained?

(A)   By holding regular training sessions

(B)   By managing companies' assets and resources

(C)   By exposing patients' medical reports without their consent

(D)   By withdrawing sound confidential agreements

(66)   Health care is benefiting through which of the following?

(A)   Physician notes

(B)   Appointment scheduling

(C)   Electronic health records

(D)   All of the above

(67)   Which of the following statements is true regarding maintaining patients' confidentiality?

(A)   Employees in health care are subject to confidentiality clauses in their contracts.

(B)   There is no common law to maintain professional confidentiality.

(C)   The Data Protection Act does not require that patient medical records be kept safe.

(D)   Patients should not be informed about the information that is being collected about them and with whom it is shared.

(68)   Which of the following frequently requests information about the patients?

(A)   Any person from the general public

(B)   Any of the patients' acquaintances

(C)   Insurance companies

(D)   All of the above

(69)   Which of the following is a characteristic of random sampling?

(A)   Each observation from the population has an equal chance of being included in the study.

(B)   It ensures an equal probability of inclusion in the sample for each sample unit.

(C)   Samples are taken in locations that are convenient for the sampler.

(D)   It is a way of taking samples from the population that can be divided into subpopulations.

(70) Which of the following are ways to protect patient confidentiality?

(A) Development of sound policies and confidential agreements

(B) Provision of regular training

(C) Storage of all the data on secure systems

(D) All of the above

(71) In health data management, the model for improvement is used for which of the following purpose?

(A) To emphasize the importance of measurement in improvement efforts

(B) To provide monetary benefits to the organization

(C) To provide information regarding the organization's employees' routines

(D) None of the above

(72) Data collection includes which of the following tasks?

(A) Analyzing data

(B) Monitoring data

(C) Updating data

(D) Monetizing data

(73)   Which of the following is a characteristic of clustered sampling?

(A)   Each observation from the population has an equal chance of being included in the study.

(B)   It ensures an equal probability of inclusion in the sample for each sample unit.

(C)   It is used when populations naturally group themselves into clusters.

(D)   It is a way of taking samples from the population that can be divided into subpopulations.

(74)   What does the management of data refer to?

(A)   A company's willingness to invest in data

(B)   Improving patient outcomes

(C)   Lowering health-care costs

(D)   Maintaining records on a physical asset

(75)   Which of the following is a characteristic of stratified sampling?

(A)   Each observation from the population has an equal chance of being included in the study.

(B)   It ensures an equal probability of inclusion in the sample for each sample unit.

(C)   Samples are taken in locations that are convenient for the sampler.

(D)   It is a way of taking samples from the population that can be divided into subpopulations.

Performance and Process Improvement Questions

(76)   PDSA is a problem-solving technique. What does PDSA stand for?

(A)   Plan-Do-Study-Act

(B)   Platelet Disorder Support Association

(C)   People's Dispensary for Sick Animals

(D)   Player Development Soccer Academy

(77)   Which of the following ensures the best execution of health-care distribution in a health-care organization?

(A)   The hospital's experience

(B)   Teamwork

(C)   Individual performance

(D)   None of the above

(78)   How can you ensure patient-centric improvements in health care?

(A)   Increase the number of patients.

(B)   Admit patients with different diseases

(C)   Increase staff members

(D)   Honor and respect the patients' choices

(79) _____ is the extent to which clinical services advance the strategic directions of an organization.

(A)   Clinical impact

(B)   Strategic fit

(C)   Academic commitments

(D)   All of the above

(80)   Which of the following groups of individuals is part of a core team?

(A)   Doctors

(B)   Nurses

(C)   Pharmacists

(D)   All of the above

(81)   Who was the first person to propose the Plan-Do-Check-Act (PDCA)?

(A)   Walter Shewhart

(B)   William Shakespeare

(C)   Albert Einstein

(D)   W. Edwards Deming

(82) What is the percentage of productivity that the process of Six Sigma is expected to provide?

(A)   100%

(B)   99.99%

(C)   99.99966%

(D)   50%

(83) Understanding root causes for variations and defects is the other name for _____.

(A)   Analysis

(B)   Training

(C)   Education

(D)   Certification

(84) Which of the following individuals is considered a champion in a health-care setting?

(A)   A person who brings in the most patients

(B)   The doctor who treats the most patients

(C)   An employee who is devoted to improving a particular area/sector of the hospital

(D)   A nurse who works for 24 hours in the hospital

(85) According to IHI, which of the following is the primary step in the process of improvement?

(A) Leading from the front

(B) Forming a balanced team

(C) Developing action plans

(D) None of the above

(86) Which of the following best describes lean in health care?

(A) It is to go to sleep.

(B) It is a set of operating philosophies and methods.

(C) It is the other name for a core team.

(D) All of the above.

(87) Six Sigma follows the following processes:

  1. Define

  2. Control

  3. Analyze

  4. Measure

  5. Improve

Identify the processes' correct order.

(A) 2, 1, 3, 5, 4

(B) 1, 4, 3, 5, 2

(C) 1, 2, 3, 4, 5

(D) 5, 4, 3, 2, 1

(88)	Which of the following best describes a process map in health care?

(A)	It visually represents the entire project process.

(B)	It represents the map of an area where the project is to be carried out.

(C)	Both A and B.

(D)	None of the above.

(89)	Why is a work breakdown structure needed?

(A)	To increase workload

(B)	To identify nursing errors

(C)	To make decentralizing decisions

(D)	All of the above

(90)	Which of the following serves as the best medium to logically express the activities of a project?

(A)	Cell phone

(B)	Paper files

(C)	Electronic health records

(D)	Precedence diagram method

(91)   An Ishikawa diagram is a graphical plot used to estimate the causes of an effect. What is another name for an Ishikawa diagram?

(A)   Fishbone diagram

(B)   Precedence diagram

(C)   Six Sigma plot

(D)   None of the above

(92)   Which of the following is a benefit of a fishbone diagram?

(A)   It identifies the number of lazy nurses in the hospital.

(B)   It identifies the number of critically ill patients in the hospital.

(C)   It identifies the areas in the hospital's system that need improvement.

(D)   It provides the demands of the customers/patients.

(93)   What does HFMEA stand for in health care?

(A)   Healthcare Failure Mode and Effect Analysis

(B)   Human Failure Mitigation and Extension Activities

(C)   Both A and B

(D)   None of the above

(94)   The questionnaire that assesses teams is based on _____ dimensions.

(A)   Seven

(B)   Ten

(C)   One

(D)   Eight

(95) Which of the following is one of the dimensions of the questionnaire that assesses teams?

(A)   Problem-solving ability

(B)   Financial constraints

(C)   Individual experience

(D)   Number of members

(96) Proper documentation of results is essential after analysis. Identify a feature of good documentation from the following:

(A)   Inspires confidence

(B)   Has the greatest number of pages

(C)   Increases feasibility for future enhancement

(D)   Both A and C

(97) Why is clinical education important in health care?

(A)   To create a good impression on the patient

(B)   To educate future health-care professionals

(C)   To create a good impression on the boss

(D)   All of the above

(98)   Why is the use of an action plan vital?

(A)   To ensure continuous improvement

(B)   To protect nurses and staff from developing laziness

(C)   Both A and B

(D)   None of the above

(99)   Which of the following are the advantages of hiring champions in a health-care setting?

(A)   They deliver top-quality care.

(B)   They improve employee motivation and retention.

(C)   They identify gaps and errors in the ways an organization does things.

(D)   All of the above.

(100)   Which of the following is the Act stage in PDCA?

(A)   Changes in documents are made.

(B)   Information is evaluated.

(C)   Plans are put in motion.

(D)   None of the above.

(101)   For a better analysis and assessment, it is essential to observe the performance of each of the team members in detail. Which of the following is the best way to keep track of those observations?

(A)   Memorize them

(B)   Document them properly

(C)   Share them with a fellow team member

(D)   None of the above

(102)   Which of the following should be used as a metric for success in improvement initiatives?

(A)   Safety

(B)   Financial results

(C)   Number of patients

(D)   Number of staff members

(103)   Which of the following best describes the Six Sigma process?

(A)   Lean

(B)   Management tool

(C)   Action plan

(D)   Success

(104) _____ needs to be measured in the Six Sigma process to increase the quality of a process's outputs.

(A)   Number of patients

(B)   Errors

(C)   Defects

(D)   Efficiency

(105) Communication is essential in _____ steps of the improvement process.

(A)   Three

(B)   The last four

(C)   All

(D)   Zero

(106) Stakeholders have a view of a health-care setting and its improvement processes. Where can this view be used?

(A)   In assessing success

(B)   In assessing failures

(C)   In assessing processes

(D)   None of the above

(107) If an emergency situation occurs in a hospital, which of the following teams needs to take action immediately?

(A)   Contingency teams

(B)   Core teams

(C)   Coordinating teams

(D)   Ancillary teams

(108) Quality of health care can be gauged by assessing its structure, processes and outcomes. Who proposed this idea?

(A)   Avedis Donabedian

(B)   Vivian Thomas

(C)   Walker Percy

(D)   James Parkinson

(109) What does TQM stand for?

(A)   Total quality management

(B)   Training quota manager

(C)   Both A and B

(D)   None of the above

(110)   A process is carried out in a health-care system but fails to achieve the desired results. Which of the following analyses can be carried out to prevent the process's failure the next time?

(A)   Failure mode and effect analysis

(B)   Total quality analysis

(C)   Root cause analysis

(D)   Individual analysis

(111)   For which of the following purposes can process mapping data be used?

(A)   To redesign clinical pathways

(B)   To locate the process

(C)   To identify the number of recovered patients

(D)   None of the above

(112) _____ is one of the basic elements of the management function.

(A)   Planning

(B)   Staffing

(C)   Organizing

(D)   All of the above

(113) _____ gives us a map of what we need to accomplish and makes it easier to stay on track.

(A)   Reverse planning

(B)   Scope statement

(C)   Root cause analysis

(D)   All of the above

(114) Which of the following is not considered a resource in health care?

(A)   People

(B)   Equipment

(C)   Material

(D)   None of the above

(115) Which of the following can provide an organization with qualitative information about individuals' performance?

(A)   General ratings

(B)   Specific ratings

(C)   Both A and B

(D)   None of the above

Patient Safety Questions

(116)   Which of the following provides the best medium for maintaining a patient's medical records?

(A)   Paper files

(B)   Cell phones

(C)   Electronic health records

(D)   None of the above

(117)   Since 1983, there have been a total of 235 reported infant abduction cases in the United States. Out of these, 117 have taken place on the premises of hospitals. Which of the following measures can reduce the number of infant kidnappings from hospitals?

(A)   Provide NICU facilities in mothers' rooms

(B)   Install a WiFi–linked security system that gives information about babies' location in real time

(C)   Hire responsible guards

(D)   Install CCTV cameras outside the rooms where babies are kept

(118)   "Patient safety is the absence of preventable harm to a patient during the process of health care and reduction of risk of unnecessary harm associated with health care to an acceptable minimum." Which organization created this definition of health care?

(A)   WHO

(B)   HQCB

(C)   IHI

(D)   IOM

(119) _____ allows health-care organizations to determine strategies that can be implemented to effectively achieve set objectives.

(A)   Training

(B)   Education

(C)   Certification

(D)   Evaluation

(120) Which of the following is the third-most responsible cause of deaths in the United States?

(A)   Diabetes

(B)   Heart attacks

(C)   Medical accidents

(D)   Cancer

(121)   Patient safety is an extremely important aspect that needs to be considered a priority in health care. To ensure the quality of patient safety, which of the following should be identified?

(A)   Errors in a hospital's patient safety programs

(B)   Errors in the programs of other hospitals compared to the errors in the hospital that is looking to overhaul its patient safety program

(C)   Both A and B

(D)   None of the above

(122)   In the United States, more than 7,000 to 9,000 people die as a result of medication errors, especially due to administration of wrong dosages in hospitals. Which of the following measures can decrease this number?

(A)   Installing smart infusion pumps

(B)   Better training of the nursing staff

(C)   Increasing the number of nurses to divide the medication duties

(D)   Assigning a single patient's medication to two nurses: one for administering the drugs and the second for verifying the correct dosage

(123)   In a hospital, who is most responsible for ensuring patient safety?

(A)   Nurses

(B)   Doctors

(C)   Legislative bodies

(D)   All of the above

(124)   What does FMEA stand for in health care?

(A)   Failure Mode and Effect Analysis

(B)   Facilities' Municipal Electric Association

(C)   Foreign Material Exclusion Area

(D)   Farmer-Managed Extension Activities

(125) A senior nurse introduces a plan to a team of nurses for ensuring a better transfer of patients from the emergency departments to the general wards without causing any harm. The team is incomplete without which of the following personnel?

(A)   The doctors assigned for the patients being transferred

(B)   The head nurse of the emergency department and the head nurse of the general wards

(C)   The head of the hospital

(D)   The receptionist

(126) A patient dies as a result of a medication error, even though your hospital has installed enough smart infusion pumps. Which of the following could have avoided this?

(A)   Failure mode and effect analysis

(B)   Root cause analysis

(C)   Better training of nurses responsible for operating the infusion pumps

(D)   Both B and C

(127) How does an electronic health record system contribute to ensuring patient satisfaction?

(A)   It helps patients track down their medical records and health needs with ease.

(B)   It acts as a status symbol and creates a good impression.

(C)   Patients do not have to carry health records like paper files.

(D)   It reduces medication errors.

(128)   Which of the following best describes the global trigger tool?

(A)   It provides an easy method to identify adverse events.

(B)   It provides an easy method to solve adverse events.

(C)   It provides an easy method to avoid adverse events.

(D)   All of the above.

(129)   To reduce patient safety risks, risk assessment and management plans are highly encouraged. Which of the following should be included in these plans?

(A)   The financial consequences

(B)   The patient-specific risks

(C)   The loopholes in health-care facilities provided

(D)   The standards of health-care organizations

(130)   The world is currently in a COVID-19 pandemic. All the patients admitted to hospitals are at a high risk of catching the deadly virus. How can hospital management reduce this risk?

(A)   Allocate separate COVID wards in the hospital for COVID-19 patients

(B)   Test paramedics for the virus and only allow in those who test negative

(C)   Only admit COVID-19 patients to the hospital

(D)   Do not let patients enter the general wards unless they test negative for COVID-19

(131) Under what circumstances can patient-doctor confidentiality be broken?

(A) When a patient allows the doctor to pass on the information

(B) When the information about a patient is harmless

(C) When a patient is no longer associated with the hospital

(D) When a patient is dead

(132) In a hospital, a nurse mishandled a wheelchair and a patient fell off. A few weeks later, a similar incident took place. _____ could have avoided the second incident.

(A) Proper training of the nurse

(B) A legitimate and reliable review of the first incident

(C) Installation of robotic wheelchairs

(D) Firing the nurse involved in the first incident

(133) Which of the following is the most common cause of medical error?

(A) Medication errors

(B) Wrong diagnosis

(C) Infections

(D) Unsterilized medical equipment

(134) How can a nurse minimize accidents with the handling of equipment in the hospital?

(A)   Do not operate any equipment without assistance from a fellow nurse

(B)   Do not operate any equipment without prior instructions

(C)   Unplug electrical equipment from the power source

(D)   Always lock the wheels of movable equipment such as wheelchairs and stretchers

(135) A patient admitted to the hospital has a history of sleepwalking. How can staff at the hospital ensure his safety?

(A)   Lock the patient in his room during the night hours

(B)   Assign a nurse to monitor the patient while he is sleeping, whether during the day or night hours

(C)   Allow a family member to stay with the patient at night

(D)   Chain the patient to his bed when he is sleeping

(136) Which of the following is a diagnosis that indicates a patient's safety is threatened?

(A)   Victim of natural disaster

(B)   Victim of domestic violence

(C)   Risk of fall

(D)   Imbalance of nutrition

(137) _____ is a principle of a highly reliable health-care organization.

(A)   The hospital staff's popularity

(B)   The number of functioning years

(C)   The absence of malfunctioning systems

(D)   The experience of paramedical staff

(138) What should a nurse's immediate response be when she sees a fire in a patient's room?

(A)   Use a fire extinguisher

(B)   Shout for help

(C)   Activate the fire alarm

(D)   Run to seek help

(139) Which of the following operating systems is best for ensuring the safety of infants in a hospital?

(A)   Stand-alone operating systems

(B)   Embedded operating systems

(C)   Network operating systems

(D)   None of the above

(140) _____ helps people view systems from a larger perspective, including overall structures.

(A)   Overview

(B)   Systems thinking

(C)   Education

(D)   Training

Test 1 Answers

Organizational Leadership Answers

(1)   (C) Statutory obligations.

Statutory obligations are laws currently in place that the state or federal government established. With these obligations, nothing ever changes until new laws are passed. *Statutory* means obligations with statutes, laws or regulations. *Obligation* means being morally or legally bound to follow the laws or regulations.

(2)   (D) Practice management system, patient engagement and care coordination software.

Health-care institutions must operate efficiently and systematically. Streamlining the process involves monitoring, improving and assessing the care provided to patients. Health-care reform aims to provide better results for health-care consumers; this can be accomplished by upgrading health-care practices. With the implementation of a practice management system, patient engagement and care coordination software, organizations can utilize better health processes that are accurate and useful, and that improve the system.

(3)   (A) Unit leader.

The unit leader has the responsibility of designing and implementing the strategic planning process within an organization. The process must be programmable, all-inclusive, organized and rational. Strategic planning serves to guide all organizations, including health-care organizations. Each part of the organization follows its own strategic plan.

(4)   (B) People working in the organization.

Best practices are internal practices promoted by people working in an organization. To improve the organization's overall performance, it is imperative to identify the activities that ensure these employees outperform the rest in their respective roles.

(5)   (C) Safety, effectiveness and efficiency.

The objective of quality improvement in health care is to improve effectiveness and refine the efficiency of health care for the betterment and safety of the organization and its consumers. A sound health-care system focuses on safety, effectiveness and efficiency.

(6)   (A) Kurt Lewin.

Kurt Lewin designed Lewin's change management model, a three-phase model to break a complex task down into manageable steps. Change management models can help health-care providers navigate a constantly evolving corporate world. These models can serve as a guide that helps them navigate difficult situations.

(7)   (D) Health Insurance Portability and Accountability Act (HIPAA).

HIPAA requires all health-care organizations to adhere to standards when collecting sensitive patient information. HIPAA is a federal law that regulates health-care establishments. All organizations are required to establish HIPAA-compliance programs, which are responsible for protecting health information both physically and through network security measures.

(8)   (A) Promoting healthy behavior that reduces diseases and deaths.

A health promotion program aims to engage and influence individuals and communities and make changes that decrease the risk of chronic illnesses and other morbidities. Health promotion strategies can change social, economic and environmental conditions that determine health. According to research and case studies from around the world, health promotion is effective.

(9)   (D) Unfreeze.

The first step in managing change according to Lewin's approach is unfreezing a current process to find out how it can be improved. The process helps all employees in an organization understand the urgency of change. Until you break down the existing system, you will not be able to build a new system. The key is to develop a compelling message showing why the existing way cannot last.

(10) (C) Framework for employers to stay updated with needed health-care reforms.

With the PPACA, an employer can stay updated on the health-care reforms necessary in an organization. This reduces the uncertainty concerning health insurance.

(11) (B) Legal requirements provided through a procurator.

Regulations are enacted by a body appointed by the government in conjunction with the legislative process of issuing and enforcing the regulations. In addition to enforcing the laws that protect patients' safety, they are also responsible for setting the basic quality standards.

(12) (B) Patients and doctors.

Nurses are an essential link between patients and doctors. Health-care nurses do more than just care for individual patients. For years, they have been at the forefront of major technological advances and health-care reforms.

(13) (A) Electronic medical records.

Electronic medical records (EMR) are a user-centric approach for keeping patient records. A patient's paper chart is converted to an electronic format known as an electronic health record, or an electronic medical record. EMRs are real-time records that make information available instantly.

(14) (D) Organizations' employees.

The Medicare compliance department requires the participation of all employees within the organization. It ensures that the organization meets all statutory and regulatory requirements in compliance with CMS. Implementing Medicare compliance programs requires coordination between all departments.

(15)   (B) Strategy, structure and systems.

McKinsey's 7-S Model has seven elements: strategy, structure, system, shared values, style, staff and skills. The first three elements are known as hard elements, and the rest of them are soft. Management can easily identify and influence the hard elements.

(16)   (B) Putting theory into practice.

The effectiveness of a change agent depends on the individual's ability to translate theories into practice, and this is essential to improving the quality of health-care services. Health-care organizations rely on the change agent for decision-making and to stay on top of every aspect of the organization's operations. In most instances, the change agent is an internal source or the manager of the organization.

(17)   (C) Plan, do, study and act.

PDSA, or Plan-Do-Study-Act, is a problem-solving cycle that consists of four steps for improving a process or implementing change: plan, do, study and act. Identifying the problem, implementing a solution, analyzing the results and implementing it on a larger scale is inherent in a quality improvement process.

(18)   (D) Systematically improving how medications are used.

Medication utilization analysis (MUE) helps hospitals evaluate and improve their use of medications as part of a structured or mandated multidisciplinary program.

(19)   (C) Government and public health organizations.

Both government and public health-care organizations must follow OSHA standards. These regulations are meant to keep the workplace safer, reducing the risk of injuries and diseases.

(20)   (B) It enables employees to perceive and understand the need for change.

The nudge theory targets employees of a health-care organization for the sake of moving work behavior toward a desired change. This theory relies on evidence-based indirect or subtle suggestions that lead employees to accept the change being implemented.

(21)   (A) An incident that results in death, permanent harm or severe temporary harm to a patient.

Sentinel events occur when patients die or are permanently injured because of circumstances outside their control. These circumstances are not usually associated with any underlying health condition. Reporting any patient safety event that fits the Joint Commission's definition of a sentinel event is strongly encouraged but not required.

(22)   (B) Commitment and dedication to your profession.

Certifications provide documentation that shows that you are competent in your field and knowledgeable about your organization's tools and processes. Certifications let employers know that you are open to continuous learning and improvement.

(23)   (B) Emotional reactions rather than rational objections as a response to change.

An organization in the health-care industry must understand that emotional reactions rather than pragmatic ones are commonly encountered in response to change. There are stages of emotions, such as denial, anger, depression and shock. A health-care organization must understand and empathize with its employees' situation for the change to be implemented effectively.

(24)   (C) Empathize, understand and help the workers.

Health-care organizations need to empathize with their employees' emotional states when introducing change within an organization so they can implement the change effectively. When an organization values its employees' emotions, the employees will in turn support the organization. This model is great for small organizations, but it is not suitable for companies dealing with large-scale changes.

(25)   (C) It prepares the organization to deal with resistance.

Health-care organizations can prepare themselves for the challenge of dealing with resistance by using change management models. Using these models will make their efforts to achieve the desired results easier.

(26)   (A) Practices introduced by employees of the organization.

Employees within an organization introduce internal best practices, which can be identified and used as an effective way to improve overall performance. To identify internal best practices, it is important to know those practices that contribute to the company's top-performing areas.

(27)   (B) The staff members.

Health-care organizations achieve their success through the hard work and dedication of their staff members. Each member of the staff is responsible for accomplishing a specific duty or responsibility. The goal of any health-care organization is to provide the best possible health care to patients.

(28)   (C) Monitoring patient health.

Monitoring a patient's progress is nursing's most important responsibility. Nurses stay with patients through all stages of illness, keeping a watchful eye day in and day out, while physicians tend to only check on patients from time to time.

(29)   (B) Awareness, desire, knowledge, ability and reinforcement.

Change under the ADKAR model relies on the people in front of the change. This change model reduces employee resistance that could sabotage implementation. This speeds up the change process.

(30)   (D) Denial, anger, bargaining, depression and acceptance.

Change is difficult to implement because humans have an innate tendency to resist it. Health-care organizations need to be aware of this and prepare themselves to handle this through the Kübler-Ross Change Curve's five stages, which are denial, anger, bargaining, depression and acceptance.

(31) (C) Safeguard life and give quality assurance.

Through working with health-care organizations, national and regional health authorities and other key stakeholders, DNV GL's goal is to enhance health-care quality, make it safer and support patient-centered care. A world leader in automotive quality control, DNV GL Health care helps ensure the safe and efficient movement of personnel and materials.

(32) (C) What patients get from health care.

Health-care quality has two elements: technical and functional. Technical consists of skill and accuracy in diagnosing and treating patients, while functional refers to what patients receive from the health care.

(33) (D) To measure patients' experience.

Service quality is influenced by patients' attitudes toward the services they receive, such as their preferences and opinions. A study conducted by Parasuraman et al. addressing these shortcomings resulted in the SERVQUAL scale becoming the most widely used tool to measure patient experiences. The scale measures patient satisfaction with respect to their perceptions and expectations.

(34) (C) The Baldrige National Quality Award.

Congress established the Baldrige National Quality Award in 1987, and it is considered the nation's highest quality award for performance excellence. Its purpose is to raise quality awareness and recognize companies with successful quality management systems. The quality award provides a great way for an organization to measure progress and identify opportunities for improvement if it seeks quality leadership.

(35)   (B) Report it to the Medicare compliance department.

If employees identify instances of noncompliance, they should immediately report them to Medicare's compliance department. Employees should also have the confidence to report fraud, abuse, ethical and privacy issues.

(36)   (B) A multisensory experience to better understand patients' conditions.

Immersive media technology, such as VR and AR, helps medical professionals better diagnose patients because it can give them a multisensory experience.

(37)   (C) Problems within the organization.

One of the most complex change management models is the McKinsey 7-S Model, which is deployed by companies that need complex changes. Using the McKinsey 7-S Model, companies that have internal issues can place an immediate focus on improving the situation.

(38)   (B) Awareness of employees' quality performance, gaps and ways to improve.

Employee performance appraisals serve as opportunities for professional development by making employees aware of their performance quality, performance gaps and opportunities for improvement. One member of the organization should assess the performance review, which should follow a standard format.

(39)   (D) There is a reduction in staff turnover and an increase in productivity and positivity in workers.

When companies consistently recognize and reward employees, staff turnover and absenteeism are unlikely to rise as employees become more bonded with the organization and appreciate it more. It has been shown that people's motivation and productivity increase when they are engaged and motivated in their profession.

(40)   (D) Analyzing and assessing the impact of training programs.

Training evaluations can be used to understand and obtain relevant information about the impact of training programs. In the 1950s, Dr. Donald Kirkpatrick developed Kirkpatrick's model to determine the effectiveness of training programs. Training staff properly creates an overall knowledgeable staff that can effectively handle themselves as employees, as well as collaborate and work as a team or independently without continuous supervision.

Health Data Analytics Answers

(41)   (A) Analyzing health-care data.

Health data management refers to the study of analyzing health-care data and managing it for the many stakeholders involved in health care. Health-care organizations and patients benefit from this work.

(42)   (B) Organization of medical data.

In addition to organizing medical data, health data management is responsible for integrating data and enabling its analysis to provide better care to patients and analyze insights to improve medical outcomes while safeguarding the data's privacy and security.

(43)   (D) Understanding the components required for health-care systems to become more effective.

Infonomics helps organizations understand the three components required for health-care systems to become more informative, effective and manageable.

(44)   (A) Measure, manage and monetize.

Infonomics consists of three Ms: measure, manage and monetize.

(45)   (D) Measurement of a company's willingness to invest in data.

Measuring data refers to measuring a company's willingness to invest in data as an asset. Health-care organizations generate data constantly throughout the system as they conduct business and provide services. After the health-care organization is aware of the true value of its data, it must manage the data by putting in place the programs, software and people required for its protection.

(46)   (C) Making decisions in health-care organizations.

Health analysis refers to the process of collecting and analyzing data so that it can be used for decision-making in a health-care organization. Among the other data sets included in health care, analytics are medical costs, patient behavior and pharmaceuticals. Health-care analytics can be beneficial on both macro and micro levels, affecting operational efficiencies, improving patient care and reducing overall costs.

(47) (A) Deliver quality care using data-driven methods.

With the help of health data measurement and analysis, providers can deliver quality care using data-driven methods; optimize their scheduling and staffing processes to minimize patient wait times; streamline processes related to making appointments, processing insurance and providing referrals; improve patient satisfaction and quality of care and use population health data combined with information about individual patients' health to identify at-risk patients.

(48) (A) Improvement of patient outcomes.

Data monetization involves more than making money. It can be used to improve patient outcomes, lower health-care costs, discover new revenue streams, improve care providers' lives and optimize services.

(49) (D) Commitment of medical practitioners not to reveal patients' medical treatment details.

Confidentiality in health care is medical practitioners' commitment not to reveal details of patients' medical treatment. This essentially means that any information patients provide to doctors and members of the administration must not be passed on to third parties, whether intentionally or not. Employees of medical centers are usually expected to maintain patient confidentiality. For this purpose, employees in health care are subject to confidentiality clauses in their contracts.

(50) (A) Ethical.

A breach of confidentiality is an ethical issue. Keeping confidentiality is a legal principle because patients should always be informed about the information that is being collected about them, for what reasons and with whom it is going to be shared. The Data Protection Act requires organizations to keep patients' personal and medical records safe.

(51)   (A) If it is required by law or public interest.

Disclosure of information without patients' consent is permissible under two circumstances: when it is required by law or is in the public interest. These instances are applicable if the patient is in a state of being unable to give consent or has explicitly refused to give consent. Moreover, an explanation for releasing information to the public usually revolves around the threat of serious harm to others.

(52)   (A) Maintaining patient confidentiality.

A doctor should always ask for a patient's consent before sharing information, as it demonstrates respect for the patient and is an essential part of good communication between both parties.

(53)   (A) Improvement of health care.

Patient data sets have increased exponentially as the standard of health care improves, the population increases and technology becomes more sophisticated.

(54)   (B) Sampling.

Sampling methodology can be used to solve the problem of trying to reach out to every individual. A sample is a subset that represents an accurate reflection of the population. This is a tricky methodology because populations can be diverse. The five main accepted methods of sampling are random sampling, systematic sampling, convenience sampling, clustered sampling and stratified sampling.

(55)   (C) Both A and B.

Health-care analysis can be beneficial on both macro and micro levels, affecting operational efficiencies, improving patient care and reducing overall costs. Health-care data analysis provides a combination of financial and administrative data, as well as information that can help improve patient care and services.

(56)   (D) By using population health data combined with information about individual patients' health.

Using population health data combined with information about individual patients' health enables hospitals to identify at-risk patients. The patient experience can be improved by improving treatment so it is delivered in a more personalized fashion. The scheduling and staffing processes can be optimized to minimize wait times. Moreover, data-driven methods can deliver quality care to patients. The processes related to making appointments, processing insurance and providing referrals can be streamlined to improve patient satisfaction and quality of care.

(57)   (A) To enable people to optimize the use of data.

Data management aims to enable people and organizations to optimize the use of data while collecting, storing, retaining and utilizing it in the most secure, efficient and cost-effective manner within the limits of policy and regulations.

(58)   (A) To gather quality evidence.

Gathering quality evidence is the basis of data collection. The health-care industry is increasingly gaining new insights by collecting data with the help of various tools.

(59)   (B) It ensures an equal probability of inclusion in the sample for each sample unit.

Systematic sampling ensures an equal probability of inclusion in the sample for each sample unit. To achieve regularity in sampling, systematic sampling follows a set of rules. Moreover, it is more convenient than random sampling.

(60)   (C) Legally binding agreement stating what information is confidential.

A confidentiality agreement is a legally binding document that states what information is confidential and cannot be shared with third parties. Everyone in an organization must agree to and abide by the agreement, understand it and sign it. The agreement should be shared with patients to demonstrate that the organization is upholding strict procedures and policies.

(61)   (C) It revolves around the threat of serious harm to others.

An explanation for releasing information to the public usually revolves around the threat of serious harm to others. It would include any information relevant to preventing or detecting disease or offenses, or prosecuting those who have voluntarily or involuntarily committed offenses.

(62)   (C) Samples are taken in locations that are convenient for the sampler.

Collecting samples by convenient means is a collection strategy in which samples are taken in locations that are convenient for the sampler. In random sampling, each observation from the population has an equal chance of being included in the study until the desired sample size is achieved. Systematic sampling ensures an equal probability of inclusion in the sample for each sample unit. In clustered sampling, populations naturally group themselves into clusters.

(63)   (A) It is a device used to collect information.

The data collection tool is a device/instrument used to collect information, such as a paper review form or computer-assisted interviewing software.

(64)   (A) Two.

Data collection is divided into quantitative and qualitative.

(65)   (A) By holding regular training sessions.

When people completely understand the reasons behind confidentiality policies and practices, they are more likely to adhere to them. It is essential to hold regular training sessions for all doctors, nurses, administrators and staff members to remind them how important the confidentiality rule is and to provide a refresher on the staff's duties and expectations.

(66)   (D) All of the above.

Health care is benefiting through physician notes, appointment scheduling, billing, insurance claims, electronic health records, health surveys, test results and prescriptions. Moreover, data management enables people and organizations to optimize the use of data while collecting, storing, retaining and utilizing it in the most secure, efficient and cost-effective manner within the limits of policy and regulations.

(67)   (A) Employees in health care are subject to confidentiality clauses in their contracts.

Since confidentiality is a legal principle, employees in health care are subject to confidentiality clauses in their contracts. The Data Protection Act requires that patients' personal and medical records be kept safe. Patients should always be informed about the information that is being collected about them and for what reasons and with whom it is going to be shared. Patients' privacy should be protected; it is imperative to inform them and remind them that they can withhold consent.

(68)   (C) Insurance companies.

Information about patients is frequently requested by insurance companies, employers or people involved with authority. Information should be disclosed only with the patient's permission and consent.

(69)   (A) Each observation from the population has an equal chance of being included in the study.

In random sampling, you choose the desired sample size and select from a population so that each observation has an equal chance of being included in the study until the desired sample size is achieved. A random sample will eliminate biases that can affect the validity of a study.

(70)   (D) All of the above.

It is important to develop sound policies and confidential agreements that cover all aspects of confidentiality. When people fully understand the reasons behind the policies and practices, they are likely to adhere to them. To maintain policies, it is important to hold regular training sessions for all doctors, nurses and staff members. When keeping patient data, it is imperative to use the highest standards of security and digital protection.

(71)   (A) To emphasize the importance of measurement in improvement efforts.

In health data management, the model for improvement emphasizes the importance of measurement in improvement efforts. Hundreds of health-care organizations in many countries have successfully used this tool to transform the way they provide care and safety to their patients, and improve health and quality outcomes.

(72)   (A) Analyzing data.

Data collection includes gathering, analyzing and interpreting different kinds of data from multiple sources. Other than this, data collection is performed for research purposes and to gather full understanding and interest. The health-care industry is increasingly gaining new insights into health care by collecting data with the help of various tools. To gather quality evidence is the basis of data collection, as it seeks to answer all the questions that are posed.

(73)   (C) It is used when populations naturally group themselves into clusters.

When populations naturally group themselves into clusters, cluster sampling is used. In this case, researchers use subgroups instead of individuals. Cluster sampling is more efficient than other methods because some work is already done: a group is already defined.

(74)   (D) Maintaining records on a physical asset.

Management of data involves an organization maintaining records on a physical asset, such as data. After a health organization has acknowledged its data's value, the next step is identifying where it comes from and how it is stored (managing data). Data management for health-care organizations means learning where the data is and understanding how to get that information into a form that can be managed.

(75)   (D) It is a way of taking samples from the population that can be divided into subpopulations.

The stratified sampling method is a way of taking samples from the population that can be divided into subpopulations. In clustered sampling, only certain clusters are used, whereas in stratified sampling, the individuals selected are random. This accounts for the major difference between these two sampling methods.

Performance and Process Improvement Answers

(76)   (A) Plan-Do-Study-Act.

Plan-Do-Study-Act (PDSA) is a problem-solving technique.

(77)   (B) Teamwork.

The hospital's experience or the individual efforts do not matter if there is no teamwork. Teamwork allows for efficient and rapid distribution of health-care services.

(78)   (D) Honor and respect the patients' choices.

You cannot make patient-centric improvements if you do not honor and respect patients' choices and demands.

(79)   (B) Strategic fit.

It requires a potential candidate to fit according to the values, goals and motives of a health-care organization.

(80)   (D) All of the above.

The core team comprises people involved in providing direct care. Pharmacists, doctors, and nurses are all responsible for providing direct assistance to patients in one way or another.

(81)   (A) Walter Shewhart.

Plan-Do-Check-Act was first proposed by Walter Shewhart in 1929. It was popularized by W. Edwards Deming in the 1950s as a learning model.

(82)   (C) 99.99966%.

Six Sigma is a management tool that promises 99.99966 percent productivity, without any defects.

(83)   (A) Analysis.

Training and education are means of transferring information from one individual to another. Certification is provided when an individual acquires a certain amount of knowledge. However, analysis allows you to identify errors and gives you an in-depth view of root causes and their variations and defects.

(84)   (C) An employee who is devoted to improving a particular area/sector of the hospital.

An employee who is dedicated to bringing positive change to a specific health-care setting is considered a champion.

(85)   (B) Forming a balanced team.

According to IHI, the Institute for Healthcare Improvement, the foremost step on the road that leads to improvement is the formation of a balanced and dedicated team.

(86)   (B) It is a set of operating philosophies and methods.

Lean is a methodology that is applied to achieve dramatic results in health-care improvement programs.

(87)   (B) 1, 4, 3, 5, 2.

Six Sigma follows the DMAIC principle: Define, Measure, Analyze, Improve, Control. Based on the list provided, these processes' order is 1, 4, 3, 5 and 2.

(88)   (A) It visually represents the entire project process.

A process map provides you with visual representations of all the minor and major processes running in the entire project. It allows you to have an in-depth analysis of the whole project.

(89)   (C) To make decentralizing decisions.

A work breakdown structure divides the work into several parts and transfers each part to different localities. This reduces the burden of making the decision from one individual, as decentralized decisions are made.

(90)   (D) Precedence diagram method.

This graphical method illustrates things with the help of nodes and arrows. Nodes signify the activities, and arrows refer to the internal links between the activities.

(91)   (A) Fishbone diagram.

A fishbone diagram, or Ishikawa diagram, is a graphical representation of the causes of a problem. Teams use these diagrams to better understand the problems in a system in order to be able to solve them effectively.

(92)   (C) It identifies the areas in the hospital's system that need improvement.

A fishbone diagram provides a graphical representation of the causes of a problem. It also helps you identify the sectors of the hospital that require attention and consequent improvement.

(93)   (A) Healthcare Failure Mode and Effect Analysis.

HFMEA is an analysis technique that is applied before the launch of a project, process or technique. This analysis identifies the potential failure points in a system and the consequences they can cause. The issues can then be resolved before the launch of the system.

(94)   (D) Eight.

There are eight dimensions to a questionnaire that assesses teams.

(95)   (A) Problem-solving ability.

The eight dimensions to a questionnaire that assesses the teams are problem-solving ability, roles, team process, skills and learning, underlying team relationships, intergroup relationships, passions and commitments, and purpose and goals.

(96)   (D) Both A and C.

The number of pages does not count, but the documentation should instill confidence in the individuals and provide feasibility for future improvements.

(97)   (B) To educate future health-care professionals.

Clinical education is incredibly important for future generations. If you yourself are not well educated about health care, you cannot educate future health-care professionals correctly.

(98)   (A) To ensure continuous improvement.

An action plan contains all the necessary actions for continuous process improvements.

(99)   (D) All of the above.

A champion in a health-care setting is an employee who is dedicated to bringing positive changes to a particular sector of the hospital. Champions also contribute to providing quality health care, motivate other employees and identify gaps in the hospital's systems.

(100)   (A) Changes in documents are made.

Changes in documents are made in the Act stage of PDCA.

(101)   (B) Document them properly.

The most professional way to keep a proper record of all of your observations is to document them properly.

(102)   (B) Financial results.

Safety is the metric for quality in health care, and financial results are the metric for success in health-care improvement initiatives.

(103)   (B) Management tool.

Six Sigma is a management tool that is used to enhance the safety and quality of health care for patients through the DMAIC mechanisms.

(104)   (D) Efficiency.

Efficiency is measured in the Six Sigma process so that errors and improvements are accurately compared for further processes.

(105)   (C) All.

Communication between staff members and patients and doctors is extremely important at all stages of the improvement process. It reduces the chances of errors and contributes greatly in maximizing the productivity of a process.

(106)   (A) In assessing success.

One of the prerequisites of assessing success is considering the view of stakeholders about your process improvements and techniques. If in your stakeholders' view, you have done a good job, it reflects your success.

(107)   (A) Contingency teams.

Contingency teams in a health-care setting are comprised of individuals who are solely responsible for handling emergency situations, such as the occurrence of a natural disaster and the patients resulting due to it. These teams must take action immediately.

(108)   (A) Avedis Donabedian.

Avedis Donabedian was a famous physicist who proposed the theory of quality of health care and said that it can be gauged by evaluating its structures, processes and results.

(109)   (A) Total quality management.

TQM is a model that involves process-based and team-based processes. It also involves transformational change, and it works to create an environment that is friendly to continuous improvements.

(110)   (A) Failure mode and effect analysis.

Failure mode and effect analysis, FMEA, is carried out before the launch of a project, technique or system. It closely identifies the potential failure points of a system, works through their consequences and proposes a solution to the identified problem to increase the efficiency of the system or the project before it is launched so that the process does not fail a second time.

(111)   (A) To redesign clinical pathways.

A process map provides an in-depth view of the processes running in a system. This can help you redesign a clinic pathway relatively easily because you are able to identify errors in the system with just a glance at the map.

(112)   (D) All of the above.

Planning, staffing and organizing are all basic elements of management function. If these elements are met, process management becomes significantly easier.

(113)   (A) Reverse planning.

Reverse planning, also called backward planning, starts with the goal that is to be achieved and then devises a plan that will lead up to achieving that goal.

(114)   (D) None of the above.

People, materials and equipment are all considered resources in health care.

(115)   (C) Both A and B.

General ratings provide an overview of an individual's performance, and specific ratings provide the quality of their performance with respect to specific areas. Both these ratings serve as qualitative information for the organization about a person's performance.

Patient Safety Answers

(116) (C) Electronic health record systems.

An electronic health record (EHR) system is a paperless and patient-centered digital solution that enables you to maintain an up-to-date history of a patient's medical conditions. All the other methods, including paper files, are time consuming and inefficient to maintain.

(117) (B) Install a WiFi-linked security system that gives information about babies' location in real time.

All the other methods will ensure infants' safety, but a WiFi-linked security system will allow you to locate a baby even if it has been abducted.

(118) (A) WHO.

WHO, the World Health Organization, created this definition of patient safety.

(119) (D) Evaluation.

It is only evaluation that allows for the assessment of strategies that can help in achieving set objectives. Education and training are ways of transferring the knowledge you have acquired. Certification is provided when you have attained a desired amount of knowledge.

(120) (C) Medical accidents.

According to a Johns Hopkins study, medical accidents are the third-leading cause of death in the United States.

(121) (A) Errors in a hospital's patient safety programs.

To ensure the quality of patient safety, it is important to identify errors within an organization's own safety programs instead of those of other hospitals' programs.

(122)   (A) Installing smart infusion pumps.

Even if nurses are better trained or greater in number, the chances of human error will still persist. On the other hand, smart infusion pumps administer drugs to patients in the correct dosage with just a click, thereby helping to reduce the rate of medication error.

(123)   (D) All of the above.

All the people working in a hospital are responsible for ensuring patient safety, as are legislative bodies that make the laws that govern high-quality health-care provision.

(124)   (A) Failure Mode and Effect Analysis.

FMEA stands for failure mode and effect analysis. In health care, failure mode and effect analysis allows for an approach to identify potential failure points in a system, the consequences they could lead to and the ways they could harm patient safety.

(125)   (B) The head nurse of the emergency department and the head nurse of the general wards.

These two nurses must be a part of the team to lead from the front and ensure that no mishaps occur. Without these nurses, the team is incomplete.

(126)   (A) Failure mode and effect analysis (FMEA).

Root cause analysis identifies only the root causes of the problem. Better training of nurses still leaves a chance for human error. However, the FMEA technique would have helped avoid this patient's death as a result of medication error because it allows an organization to assess the potential failure points in a system and fix them before the system is launched.

(127)   (A) It helps patients track down their medical records and health needs with ease.

Patients are most satisfied when they are continuously updated about their health needs and can easily track their medical history.

(128)   (A) It provides an easy method to identify adverse events.

A GTT allows health-care personnel to identify adverse events, which can then be solved or avoided in the future.

(129)   (B) The patient-specific risks.

If nothing else, the risk assessment and management plans should include well-documented patient-specific risks because it is the patients' safety that you need to ensure and improve through these assessments.

(130)   (B) Test paramedics for the virus and only allow in those who test negative.

Isolation of COVID-19 patients is not a measure used to protect other patients. Besides, a hospital should be welcoming to all patients. An effective safety precaution would be to test paramedics for the virus and only allow those who test negative to enter the premises.

(131)   (A) When a patient allows the doctor to pass on the information.

Even if the information is harmless or the patient is dead, confidentiality cannot be broken unless a patient asks the doctor to break it.

(132)   (B) A legitimate and reliable review of the first incident.

The foremost thing you need to do after such an incident is review it in detail. Figure out the loopholes and find what is lacking. Take measures to fix them so that the incident is not repeated.

(133)   (A) Medication errors.

Out of all the medical errors in hospitals, administering wrong medications and overdosages are the most likely to occur.

(134)   (B) Do not operate any equipment without prior instructions.

Detailed instructions from a doctor can help minimize accidents related to how medical equipment is handled. Medical personnel that has not been trained on how to operate medical equipment should not be allowed to handle it.

(135)   (B) Assign a nurse to monitor the patient while he is sleeping, whether during the day or night hours.

Chaining the patient, locking him up or relying upon family members to babysit will not lead to patient safety. Instead, a nurse should carefully monitor the patient when he is asleep.

(136)   (C) Risk of fall.

The rest of the options are not the causes of poor patient safety in a hospital.

(137)   (C) The absence of malfunctioning systems.

The absence of malfunctioning systems is a principle of a highly reliable health-care organization.

(138)   (C) Activate the fire alarm.

Activating a fire alarm will immediately send a signal to people who are responsible for putting out a fire. Thus it should be a nurse's first response if he or she sees a fire in a medical facility.

(139)   (A) Stand-alone operating systems.

Stand-alone systems are best for the security of infants in a hospital because it is not easy to hack these systems.

(140)   (B) Systems thinking.

Training and education refer to the transfer of knowledge from one individual to another. Overview enables you to skim through things, whereas systems thinking allows you to carry out in-depth research of the entire system.

Test 2

Organizational Leadership Questions

(1)   Who is the first person to act when a patient is in critical condition?

(A)   Surgeon

(B)   Nurse

(C)   Doctor

(D)   Patient's family

(2)   What does a planned change require?

(A)   An organization's good reputation

(B)   Strong government and agencies

(C)   Strong leadership and competence to implement organization-wide changes

(D)   A positive and productive staff

(3)   What do change models consist of?

(A)   Methodologies, theories and concepts

(B)   Queries, analogies and concepts

(C)   Questions, evaluation and analysis

(D)   Predictions, analogies and evaluation

(4)   How can health-care systems be improved?

(A)   By introducing improved medications

(B)   With the application of new tactics to support health-care staff

(C)   By designing efficient, affordable and sustainable health systems

(D)   By training doctors and specialists

(5)   What is the purpose of deploying external best practices?

(A)   To help patients recover quickly

(B)   To help an organization grow beyond its original setting

(C)   To expand a hospital's operating area

(D)   To increase the quality of services

(6)   What is the most important feature of good customer service?

(A)   Talking politely

(B)   Improving the hospital's image

(C)   Responding quickly to patients' queries

(D)   Engaging with customers for long hours

(7)   What is the responsibility of the employees in the complaint department?

(A)   Analyzing health-care services

(B)   Helping doctors during treatment

(C)   Answering patient queries

(D)   Receiving complaints, collecting complaint data and passing it on to those with the authority to act upon it

(8)   What is strongly encouraged but not required to be reported to the Joint Commission?

(A)   Rudeness

(B)   Incompetence

(C)   Reporting of sentinel events

(D)   Lateness

(9)   What does medical documentation consist of?

(A)   A patient's physical attributes

(B)   Information about a patient's care, including treatment and diagnosis

(C)   Only medical history

(D)   Medical history of a patient's family

(10)   What does a change agent supervise?

(A)   Patients' documentation

(B)   Patient feedback

(C)   Overall change in a health-care organization

(D)   Treatments in a health-care organization

(11)   What is the aim of health-care quality improvement training programs?

(A)   Increasing treatment efficiency

(B)   Documenting patient treatment strategies

(C)   Preparing medical residents for quality improvement and patient safety

(D)   Preparing doctors to handle sentinel events

(12)   Why are employers leveraging certification?

(A)   They want to hire the best-qualified individuals to contribute to the quality of care patients receive.

(B)   It is a good way to earn money for organizations.

(C)   It helps employers protect patients during treatment.

(D)   It helps the organization develop systematic facilities.

(13)   How should an accreditation source be selected?

(A)   It must reflect the social responsibility of the patients.

(B)   It must reflect doctors' needs.

(C)   It must reflect an organization's vision and mission.

(D)   It must reflect the requirements of the government.

(14)   What are the principles that ISO 9001 follows?

(A)   Patients' ethical principles

(B)   Project management principles

(C)   Staff members' responsibility principles

(D)   Quality management principles

(15)   What is the responsibility of the privacy and security department?

(A)   It protects electronic and nonelectronic patient records.

(B)   It is responsible for employee conduct.

(C)   It provides security to employers.

(D)   It provides help and safety to a patient's family.

(16)   What is the ethics and compliance department responsible for?

(A)   Maintaining staff ethics and integrity

(B)   Providing security to staff and maintaining their ethics

(C)   Looking after the moral obligations of the organization

(D)   Creating and maintaining codes of business conduct and processing the disclosure of conflicts of interest

(17)   The AHRQ has divided the process of implementation of best practices into how many stages?

(A)   Two

(B)   Three

(C)   Four

(D)   Six

(18)   What are the soft elements of the McKinsey 7-S Model?

(A)   Sustainability, skills, staff and shared values

(B)   Values, responsibility, ethics and sustainability

(C)   Shared values, style, staff and skills

(D)   Style, staff, values and strategy

(19)   What is the Baldrige criteria used for?

(A)   To determine the demand for medications

(B)   To evaluate performance, improve quality and help organizations be efficient

(C)   To determine the performance of doctors

(D)   To evaluate the competence of doctors

(20)   What does it mean when an organization claims to be ISO 9001-certified?

(A)   Standards have been implemented by agencies.

(B)   Standards have been inspected by the government.

(C)   Standards have been audited, reviewed and approved by a qualified party.

(D)   Standards have been met pertaining to patients' requirements.

(21)   Which hospital program was developed in December 1990 by the Board of Directors of the American Nurses Association (ANA)?

(A)   The Baldrige Criteria for Performance program

(B)   An accrediting and standards-setting program

(C)   A Magnet Hospital Recognition Program for Excellence in Nursing Services

(D)   A quality control management program

(22)   What is the responsibility of the internal audit and investigation department?

(A)   To secure and maintain records

(B)   To enforce disciplinary standards

(C)   To ensure and inspect internal operations

(D)   To maintain codes of business conduct

(23)   What is the purpose of compliance effectiveness surveys?

(A)   To allow compliance leaders to focus on patients' treatment and effectiveness

(B)   To allow compliance leaders to gain insight into the program's effectiveness and measure its performance

(C)   To allow compliance leaders to protect the integrity of patient reports

(D)   To allow compliance leaders to gain information about the organization's effectiveness

(24)   How many stages is the Bridges' Transition Model theory divided into?

(A)   Eight

(B)   Twelve

(C)   Three

(D)   Four

(25)   What is the aim of a patient representative?

(A)   To represent a patient's mental health condition

(B)   To represent a patient's illness

(C)   To represent a patient's needs, concerns and expectations to the health-care organization

(D)   To convey a patient's feedback about treatment

(26)   What is the purpose of evaluating for compliance in internal and external requirements?

(A)   Monitoring and auditing the health-care organization

(B)   Detecting compliance risks inherent in an organization's operations

(C)   Identifying what works well in a program and what can be improved

(D)   Meeting the expectations of regulatory bodies

(27)   Who should always be a part of an effective quality improvement committee?

(A)   A patient representative

(B)   Doctors

(C)   A government representative

(D)   Patients

(28)   What does the Civil Rights department working under HHS regulate?

(A)   Laws and reforms for patient treatment

(B)   Staff members' mental health

(C)   Patients' treatment and health

(D)   Privacy and security rules

(29)   What is the principle of care coordination?

(A)   Dealing with a patient's family during difficult times

(B)   Dealing with doctors throughout a patient's treatment

(C)   Dealing with nurses to help a patient's family

(D)   Dealing with patients with chronic conditions

(30)　What is the implementation of clinical practice guidelines?

(A)　Advancing clinical practice by establishing standards of care

(B)　Providing patients with services that exceed their expectations

(C)　Providing new equipment to doctors

(D)　Discovering new methods of treatments

(31)　What is the purpose of education on quality improvement?

(A)　To focus on the construct of interest

(B)　To improve knowledge and skills

(C)　To increase efficiency

(D)　To increase quality assurance

(32)　What are the goals behind developing Medicare compliance programs?

(A)　To manage an organization's resources

(B)　To prevent, detect and correct noncompliance

(C)　To evaluate, detect and decrease the number of errors per treatment

(D)　To analyze, increase and implement efficiency

(33)　What is the dissemination of information within an organization?

(A)　The method by which information is deleted

(B)　The method by which information is organized

(C)　The method by which information is stored

(D)　The method by which information is distributed to the public

(34)   In some instances, who is allowed to act without seeking permission from the doctor?

(A)   Staff members

(B)   Surgeons

(C)   Nurses

(D)   Health-care workers

(35)   What is meant by health-care utilization?

(A)   Improving health care

(B)   Transferring the information, responsibility and authority of the patient

(C)   A person using services to prevent and treat health problems

(D)   Managing the gaps in patient care

(36)   What quality improvement method was developed in 1999 by the Institute of Medicine?

(A)   Six Sigma quality improvement method

(B)   STEEP quality improvement method

(C)   Pareto diagrams quality improvement method

(D)   PDSA quality improvement method

(37)   What are the five stages of carrying out projects?

(A)   Initiate, plan, execute, monitor and conclude

(B)   Analyze, evaluate, monitor, implement and conclude

(C)   Study, brainstorm, plan, evaluate and execute

(D)   Survey, review, conclude, evaluate and execute

(38)   What are the four levels of Kirkpatrick's model to examine training programs?

(A)   Study, survey, explore and judge

(B)   Learn, define, analyze and evaluate

(C)   Check, appraise, inspect and effect

(D)   Reaction, learning, behavior and result

(39)   Who can offer licensure?

(A)   Health organizations

(B)   Nongovernmental offices

(C)   Agency or government offices

(D)   Government offices

(40)   What is the function of nanomedicine?

(A)   To improve health care at the molecular level

(B)   To create medical tools

(C)   To better understand the condition of patients

(D)   To reduce treatment time

Health Data Analytics Questions

(41)   Why is it important to decide which data collection tool to use?

(A)   To streamline processes related to making appointments, processing insurance and providing referrals

(B)   To optimize scheduling and staffing processes

(C)   To deliver quality care using data-driven methods

(D)   To conduct research most efficiently

(42)   Which of the following statements is true about phenomenology?

(A)   It is the study of human societies.

(B)   It helps in understanding how people live their lives.

(C)   It is used to explore social interactions within human relationships.

(D)   It discusses people's experiences with some events.

(43)   Why have organizations started to rely on intangible assets?

(A)   To create value

(B)   To create wealth

(C)   To gain reputation

(D)   None of the above

(44)   The task of data management covers which of the following factors?

(A)   Data being created across multiple data tiers

(B)   Cloud storage and on-premises storage

(C)   Ensuring the security and privacy of the data

(D)   All of the above

(45)   On which of the following factors does the type of data produced within the health system depend?

(A)   Patient experience

(B)   Hospital response

(C)   Treatment or therapy

(D)   All of the above

(46)   Which of the following methods is used to measure reactions to unusual occurrences?

(A)   Phenomenology

(B)   Participant observation

(C)   Ethnography

(D)   Interviews

(47) In which of the following data collection methods do we look at the information in greater detail?

(A) Qualitative method

(B) Quantitative method

(C) Both A and B

(D) None of the above

(48) What is the process of using graphics to present information called?

(A) Data warehousing

(B) Data mining

(C) Data visualization

(D) None of the above

(49) Which of the following statements accurately describes operational dashboards?

(A) They provide real-time results of what is occurring within a hospital setting.

(B) They show patterns and trends over time.

(C) They can be used to provide data on a broader scale.

(D) All of the above.

(50) Which of the following are the most common visualization tools?

(A) Charts

(B) Tables

(C) Graphs

(D) All of the above

(51)   Which of the following statements accurately describes analytical dashboards?

(A)   They provide real-time results of what is occurring within a hospital setting.

(B)   They show patterns and trends over time.

(C)   They can be used to provide data on a broader scale.

(D)   All of the above

(52)   Which of the following is a method used in grounded theory?

(A)   Participant observation

(B)   Interviews

(C)   Document or artifact collection

(D)   All of the above

(53)   Which of the following purposes are evaluation techniques used for?

(A)   To determine a program's success

(B)   To extract useful patterns from the data

(C)   Both A and B

(D)   None of the above

(54)   Which of the following factors should be included in the assessment process?

(A)   Questions

(B)   Measures

(C)   Approaches to assessing

(D)   All of the above

(55)   Which of the following is an accepted method of sampling?

(A)   Random sampling

(B)   Convenience sampling

(C)   Clustered sampling

(D)   All of the above

(56)   What can be an excellent means of communicating information so that the community will be influencing policy decisions?

(A)   Evaluation

(B)   Optimization

(C)   Management

(D)   All of the above

(57)   Which of the following statements accurately describes strategic dashboards?

(A)   They provide real-time results of what is occurring within a hospital setting.

(B)   They show patterns and trends over time.

(C)   They can be used to provide data on a broader scale.

(D)   All of the above.

(58)   Which of the following statements is true about ethnography?

(A)   Anthropology defines ethnography as the study of human societies.

(B)   It does not help in understanding how people live their lives.

(C)   It is used to explore social interactions within human relationships.

(D)   It discusses people's experiences with some events.

(59)   On which of the following does quality management rely?

(A)   Statistical tools

(B)   Data management

(C)   Data measurement

(D)   None of the above

(60)   Which of the following techniques is used as a quality tool for problem-solving, process improvement and performance measurement?

(A)   Data collection

(B)   Analysis

(C)   Both A and B

(D)   None of the above

(61)   Which of the following accurately describes the participant observation method of grounded theory?

(A)   It is the study of human societies and cultures.

(B)   It discusses people's experiences with some events.

(C)   Researchers study subjects by observing.

(D)   Its purpose is to gather data from subjects on a wide variety of topics.

(62)   What does qualitative data collection refer to?

(A)   Data in the form of words

(B)   Data that includes observations and descriptions

(C)   Data in nonnumerical form

(D)   All of the above

(63)   Which of the following two graphs combine to make the Pareto chart?

(A)   Bar graphs and line graphs

(B)   Bar graphs and area graphs

(C)   Line graphs and area graphs

(D)   None of the above

(64)   Which of the following statements is true about qualitative data collection methods?

(A)   It looks at the information in greater detail.

(B)   It lends a lower understanding to the raw data.

(C)   It does not evaluate psychological factors.

(D)   It deals with something that can be counted.

(65)   Which of the following statements is true about line graphs?

(A)   They represent the percentage of defects for a specific period.

(B)   Bar graphs combine with line graphs to create the Pareto chart.

(C)   Both A and B

(D)   None of the above

(66) Which of the following accurately describes the interview method of grounded theory?

(A) It is the study of human societies and cultures.

(B) It discusses people's experiences with events.

(C) Researchers study subjects by observing.

(D) Its purpose is to gather data from subjects on a wide variety of topics.

(67) Which of the following can be used to carry out primary data collection?

(A) Data collection tools

(B) Data warehousing techniques

(C) Both A and B

(D) None of the above

(68) Which of the following is the most-used qualitative data collection method?

(A) Ethnography

(B) Grounded theory

(C) Phenomenology

(D) All of the above

(69) Which of the following accurately describes the document or artifact collection method of grounded theory?

(A) It is the study of human societies and cultures.

(B) It discusses people's experiences with some events.

(C) Researchers study subjects by observing.

(D) None of the above.

(70) Which of the following statements accurately describes the advantage of a data management platform?

(A) It helps deliver quality care using data-driven methods.

(B) It helps optimize staffing processes.

(C) It is used by companies to achieve financial benefits.

(D) It enables large companies to collect tiers of data efficiently.

(71) What does quantitative data collection refer to?

(A) Data in the form of words

(B) Data measured in the form of numbers

(C) Data in nonnumerical form

(D) None of the above

(72)   Health-care data analysis provides a combination of which two kinds of data?

(A)   Administrative and financial data

(B)   Financial and statistical data

(C)   Monetary and statistical data

(D)   None of the above

(73)   Which of the following statements is true about grounded theory?

(A)   It is the study of human societies.

(B)   It helps in understanding how people live their lives.

(C)   It is used to explore social interactions within human relationships.

(D)   It discusses people's experiences with some events.

(74)   What does visualizing data refer to?

(A)   Optimizing scheduling and staffing processes to minimize patient waiting times

(B)   Streamlining processes related to making appointments, processing insurance and providing referrals

(C)   Improving treatment in a more personalized fashion

(D)   Using graphics to present information

(75)   Data collection was designed for which of the following purposes?

(A)   Capturing useful evidence

(B)   Improving patients' health

(C)   Improving organizations' financial resources

(D)   Dealing with patients' medical records

Performance and Process Improvement Questions

(76)   Which of the following methodological processes is expected to provide 99.99966% productivity?

(A)   Root cause analysis

(B)   Six Sigma

(C)   Total quality management

(D)   PDSA

(77)   Which of the following is the accepted concept of teamwork across the world?

(A)   It is a crucial capability for constructing a more effective and patient-oriented health-care delivery system.

(B)   The number of team members is directly proportional to the quality of teamwork produced.

(C)   Both A and B.

(D)   None of the above.

(78)   Which of the following methodologies was introduced by Walter Shewhart?

(A)   PDSA

(B)   PDCA

(C)   HFMEA

(D)   RCA

(79) Identify the percentage by which teamwork lowers medical errors.

(A) 34%

(B) 25%

(C) 100%

(D) 40%

(80) Which of the following scenarios encourages and motivates physicians to get more involved in patient care?

(A) Greater number of staff members

(B) Smaller number of staff members

(C) Staff members working together

(D) Staff members working individually

(81) _____ are not included in core teams in a health-care setting.

(A) Doctors

(B) Case managers

(C) Pharmacists

(D) None of the above

(82)   Which of the following is/are the roles of a coordinating team of a health-care setting?

(A)   Providing operational management

(B)   Ensuring coordination of functions

(C)   Both A and B

(D)   None of the above

(83)   Which of the following processes uses the DMAIC methodology?

(A)   Six Sigma

(B)   FMEA

(C)   RCA

(D)   PDSA

(84)   Which of the following is a DMAIC methodology step?

(A)   Act

(B)   Define

(C)   Call

(D)   Increase

(85)   Financial results should be used as a metric of _____ in health-care improvement programs.

(A)   Quality

(B)   Failure

(C)   Success

(D)   Safety

(86)   If an administrative problem arises in a hospital, which team should immediately take action?

(A)   Coordinating team

(B)   Ancillary team

(C)   Support services group

(D)   Contingency team

(87)   Fishbone diagrams are also called _____.

(A)   Ishikawa diagrams

(B)   Sequence diagrams

(C)   Ladder diagrams

(D)   Block diagrams

(88)   Health-care quality is defined by the _____ as a multidimensional standard of excellence.

(A)   World Health Organization

(B)   Institute for Healthcare Improvement

(C)   Health-Care Organization

(D)   Health Foundation

(89)   A team wants to analyze data regarding a patient's medical history. Which of the following could serve the team as a reliable source of information?

(A)   A nurse's word of mouth

(B)   The patient's electronic health record

(C)   The patient's word of mouth

(D)   None of the above

(90)   What does HFMEA stand for in health care?

(A)   Healthcare Failure Mode and Effect Analysis

(B)   Human Fertilization Modality Excellence Association

(C)   Both A and B

(D)   None of the above

(91)   Identify one of the six pillars of quality health care from the following:

(A)   Patient-centered

(B)   Number of patients

(C)   Number of staff members

(D)   Popularity in the community

(92)   How can the health disparities among ethnic minority groups be reduced?

(A)   By including staff members from these groups

(B)   By designing a mechanism that allows for equitable distribution of health-care facilities across the board

(C)   By cutting off these groups

(D)   All of the above

(93)   A hospital initiated a health-care improvement program. It failed to produce the desired outcomes. Which of the following analyses can help improve the program's results next time?

(A)   Failure mode and effect analysis

(B)   Total quality management

(C)   An action plan

(D)   Root cause analysis

(94)   Which of the following individuals may prove best suited for an effective team in a health-care setting?

(A)   Members with different backgrounds

(B)   Members with varied skills

(C)   Members with the best references

(D)   Both A and B

(95)   Which of the following best describes clinical impact?

(A)   The importance of clinical education

(B)   The clinical requirements of a community

(C)   The service volumes needed to ensure safe and effective care

(D)   None of the above

(96)   Which of the following scientists made the PDCA popular as a learning model in the 1950s?

(A)   W. Edwards Deming

(B)   Avedis Donabedian

(C)   Walter Shewhart

(D)   Albert Einstein

(97) _____ is a part of the planning phase in PDCA.

(A) Evaluation of information

(B) Implementation of policies

(C) Assessment of current procedures

(D) Documentation changes

(98) Who is considered a champion in a health-care setting?

(A) The doctor who earns the most

(B) An employee who is dedicated to improving a specific sector of the health-care setting

(C) The patient who recovers in the shortest time

(D) The most experienced nurse

(99) Which of the following provides an insight into the systems and processes initiated for health-care improvement?

(A) Bar graph

(B) Scatter graph

(C) Process map

(D) Line graph

(100) What does WBS stand for in a health-care improvement initiative?

(A) Work breakdown structure

(B) World's business school

(C) World business satellite

(D) Web-based system

(101) What do the nodes signify in a precedence diagram method?

(A) Link between activities

(B) Errors

(C) Activities

(D) Resources

(102) What should be determined first when reverse planning?

(A) The goal

(B) The method

(C) Both A and B

(D) None of the above

(103) Which of the following best describes micromanagement?

(A) Management with attention to minor details

(B) Management with deep empathy to employees

(C) Management solely focusing on major details

(D) All of the above

(104) What are the three elements of the Triple Aim in health care?

(A)   Doctors, nurses and pharmacists

(B)   Patient experience, health and cost

(C)   Doctors, nurses and patients

(D)   Number of paramedical staff, cost and patients' health

(105) Which of the following proves more helpful to the individuals on a team?

(A)   Numeric ratings

(B)   Observations

(C)   Comments

(D)   Both B and C

(106) Which of the following is/are measured under the structure attribute?

(A)   Availability of health insurance

(B)   Training of nurses

(C)   Hospital's bed capacity

(D)   All of the above

(107) What does RCA stand for in health care?

(A)   Root cause analysis

(B)   Root college of accounting

(C)   Both A and B

(D)   None of the above

(108)   Identify the graph that can be used to illustrate and explore the causes of an effect in health care.

(A)   Line graph

(B)   Precedence graph

(C)   Fishbone diagrams

(D)   All of the above

(109) Which of the following factors should be controlled to ensure the provision of quality health care?

(A)   Future process performance

(B)   Future improvements

(C)   Both A and B

(D)   None of the above

(110)   Identify the best medium to communicate the essential details and sequencing of a project to the members of a team.

(A)   Word of mouth

(B)   Detailed documents

(C)   Process maps

(D)   None of the above

(111) Identify the approach used for gathering activity resources.

(A)   Visual approach

(B)   Hierarchical approach

(C)   Radar approach

(D)   Structural approach

(112) Which of the following best describes resource estimating?

(A)   Determining the performance of resources

(B)   Logical expression of activities

(C)   Reverse planning

(D)   All of the above

(113) Reverse planning is a _____ process.

(A)   Linear

(B)   Nonlinear

(C)   Exponential

(D)   None of the above

(114) Roles and team processes are two of the _____ dimensions of a questionnaire used for assessing health-care teams.

(A)   Five

(B)   Nine

(C)   Eight

(D)   Two

(115) According to the _____, one of the primary steps in the improvement process is forming a balanced team.

(A)   IHI

(B)   HF

(C)   WHO

(D)   AMA

Patient Safety Questions

(116) What does RCA stand for in health care?

(A) Rules of common association

(B) Root cause analysis

(C) Radio corporation of America

(D) Random common access

(117) Employees must engage in patient safety programs started by an organization that _____.

(A) Has established a good reputation

(B) Has been in the business for a long time.

(C) Has a good number of experienced staff

(D) Prioritizes patient safety

(118) Which of the following best describes an adverse event?

(A) An event that causes harm to a patient

(B) An event that hampers a hospital's reputation

(C) An event that causes harm to paramedical staff

(D) An event that leads to a financial loss

(119) The absence of preventable harm to a patient during the process of health care and the reduction of risk of unnecessary harm associated with health care to an acceptable minimum is known as?

(A)   An adverse event

(B)   Medical error

(C)   Health care

(D)   Patient safety

(120) "The pursuit of methods to reduce the risk of medical errors as well as utilizing best practices for treating patients." This is the definition of patient safety according to which of the following organizations?

(A)   American Medical Association

(B)   World Health Organization

(C)   Institute for Health Care Improvement

(D)   United Nations

(121) What does ICU stand for in health care?

(A)   International computer users

(B)   Intensive care unit

(C)   Ignition control unit

(D)   Intersection capacity utilization

(122) Which of the following best describes a stand-alone system?

(A)   A system that functions independently from a network

(B)   A system that functions to help computers work together on a network

(C)   Both A and B

(D)   None of the above

(123) Heart disease and cancer are, respectively, the first- and second-leading causes of death in the United States. Which of the following is the third-leading cause of death in the country?

(A)   Car accidents

(B)   Medical errors

(C)   Alzheimer's Disease

(D)   Diabetes

(124) While fixing some medical equipment in the ICU, an electrician causes a fire. A patient is lying on the ventilator in the same room. What should be the immediate response of the nurse on duty in the ICU?

(A)   Try to extinguish the fire

(B)   Immediately remove the patient from the ICU with an oxygen supply

(C)   Wait for the orders of the doctor

(D)   Run to seek help

(125) Which of the following is not promised in hospitals' patient safety programs?

(A)   Reduction in falls

(B)   Proper medication

(C)   Resolved domestic issues

(D)   All of the above

(126) _____ is a potential risk to a patient due to poor patient safety programs in a hospital.

(A)   Depression

(B)   Falls

(C)   Medical errors

(D)   Both B and C

(127) Which of the following errors may occur while carrying out a procedure?

(A)   Wrong dose of medicine

(B)   Incorrect diagnosis

(C)   Misuse of equipment

(D)   All of the above

(128) After the occurrence of a problem in a patient safety program, what should be done to avoid the issue the next time?

(A)   Root cause analysis

(B)   Failure mode and effect analysis

(C)   Both A and B

(D)   None of the above

(129) Medical files have a risk attached to them of getting lost. Thus, _____ should replace medical files, for efficiency and patient safety.

(A)   Cell phones

(B)   Laptops

(C)   Electronic health record systems

(D)   Stand-alone systems

(130) On many occasions, equipment is responsible for a medical error. Which of the following could lead to equipment failure that the hospital staff could not be held accountable for?

(A)   Power breakdown

(B)   Equipment misuse

(C)   Use of malfunctioning equipment

(D)   All of the above

(131) How can electronic health record systems ensure the productivity of a physician?

(A) EHR systems help reduce physician workloads.

(B) EHR systems help speed up physicians' diagnosing process.

(C) EHR systems are trusted by patients.

(D) EHR systems are easier to use.

(132) _____ is an unplanned event that did not result in an injury but had the potential of causing damage.

(A) Medical error

(B) A poor diagnosis

(C) A near-miss

(D) A domestic issue

(133) Which of the following minimizes health risks and ensures a sense of safety and well-being for patients before an activity is conducted or a program is launched?

(A) Risk assessments

(B) Root cause analysis

(C) Overview of the situation

(D) Installation of embedded systems

(134) If a patient's safety is compromised in a hospital, who is held responsible?

(A)   Doctors

(B)   Governing and legislative bodies

(C)   Nurses

(D)   All of the above

(135) Medication errors account for most medical errors. To correct this problem, smart infusion pumps are being introduced in hospitals. How are these pumps ensuring better medication of patients?

(A)   As soon as you press a button, the pump automatically detects the dose a patient needs and supplies it.

(B)   A nurse selects the drug and its concentration from the list in the system of the pumps, and the medication is then infused into the patient.

(C)   Smart infusion pumps absorb extra medication if a patient is overdosed and supply more medication if a patient is underdosed.

(D)   None of the above.

(136) What does GTT stand for in health care?

(A)   Global trigger tool

(B)   Global title translation

(C)   Government technical testing

(D)   Glass torch technologies

(137)   The process of auditing, investigating, analyzing, responding and reporting an incident is called _____.

(A)   Education

(B)   Training

(C)   Review

(D)   Overview

(138)   Which of the following systems enables you to have a thorough view of a patient's complete treatment within the hospital?

(A)   Embedded system

(B)   Systems thinking

(C)   Networking system

(D)   Operating system

(139)   A culture of openness is an important principle that helps ensure safety in a health-care organization. How can a culture of openness be created?

(A)   By providing information regarding patient safety and adverse events to all patients

(B)   By having weekly meetings to address staff's personal concerns

(C)   By ensuring health-care professionals have restricted relationships with patients

(D)   None of the above

(140) What is a human-machine interface (HMI)?

(A)   It is a machine that allows you to administer drugs to a patient with a click of a button.

(B)   It is a component of a device or an application that allows humans to engage with machines.

(C)   It is a component that enables human-to-human interaction miles apart.

(D)   It is a device that links two machines.

Test 2 Answers

Organizational Leadership Answers

(1) (B) Nurse.

Health-care workers like nurses serve as a bridge between patients and health-care providers. Nurses are often the first to notice anything wrong with a patient's condition and are the first ones to act when a patient is in critical condition.

(2) (C) Strong leadership and competence to implement organization-wide changes.

Planned change should always be clearly defined with a purpose. The leader of a planned change needs to possess the knowledge and skills necessary to apply changes, both at the individual and organizational levels in a health organization.

(3) (A) Methodologies, theories and concepts.

Change models include various theories, concepts and methodologies for in-depth change in health-care organizations.

(4) (C) By designing efficient, affordable and sustainable health systems.

Health-care quality can be enhanced by designing efficient, affordable and sustainable health-care systems. This requires a variety of specialized tools and methods that assist in improving health-care quality. As determined by some measurements, the level of value delivered by a health-care resource is a measure of quality.

(5) (B) To help an organization grow beyond its original setting.

External best practices let organizations grow by looking beyond their organizational settings. In order to succeed in this competitive market, every organization needs to be aware of what its competitors are doing. By assessing how its competitors operate, an organization can improve its performance. By identifying and applying external best practices, an organization will benefit from greater capabilities and performance.

(6)   (C) Responding quickly to patients' queries.

Good customer service means taking the time to acknowledge and quickly address customer inquiries. It is one of the most important aspects of customer satisfaction.

(7)   (D) Receiving complaints, collecting complaint data and passing it on to those with authority to act upon it.

Identifying systematic problems in health care comes from studying the data compiled about negative patient visits. Complaint department employees accept patient complaints, compile data on them, then pass it on to colleagues who have decision-making authority. It has been recognized that patients' complaints are an extremely valuable resource that should be monitored and used for patient safety.

(8)   (C) Reporting of sentinel events.

The Joint Commission rules consider a sentinel event any medical event that causes death, injury or damages without primarily being related to a patient's illness or underlying problem. The Joint Commission health-care centers strongly recommend reporting any safety event that meets their definition of a sentinel event. Sentinel events are commonly occurring errors when foreign objects are retained unintentionally, falls occur and procedures are performed on the wrong patient.

(9)   (B) Information about a patient's care, including treatment and diagnosis.

Medical documentation includes patient records, medical procedures, diagnoses and treatments. Documentation must demonstrate quality care.

(10)   (C) Overall change in the health-care organization.

Change agents oversee the overall process of change in a health-care organization. They provide steady support to those whose lives are affected by changes. They also convey feedback on results achieved through change facilitation. Successfully facilitating a change is often complicated and challenging. However, a sense of accomplishment and pride is achieved when a change theory is successfully implemented.

(11)   (C) Preparing medical residents for quality improvement and patient safety.

Health-care quality improvement programs are meant to prepare medical residents to become quality improvement experts, thereby helping to ensure patient safety.

(12)   (A) They want to hire the best-qualified individuals to contribute to the quality of care patients receive.

Certification permits employers to determine which candidates exhibit the qualifications needed for success in a specific job. They wish to hire only the most qualified candidates who will contribute greatly to patient care. Certification demonstrates a candidate's desire to continue learning and growing.

(13)   (C) It must reflect an organization's vision and mission.

One must choose an accreditation source that conforms to the institutional integrity of an organization. It must be aligned with the clinical, educational and community involvement of the institution. Choosing an appropriate accreditation source for an appropriate organizational fit represents a strategic decision that merits leadership attention.

(14)   (D) Quality management principles.

ISO is an independent nongovernmental organization. A quality management system is defined in ISO 9001 as following a series of quality management principles. This standard helps companies and organizations achieve efficiency and reach their goals by facilitating conformity with a number of quality management principles.

(15)   (A) It protects electronic and nonelectronic patient records.

The privacy and security department ensures the security and confidentiality of both electronic and nonelectronic patient health information.

(16) (D) Creating and maintaining codes of business conduct and processing the disclosure of conflicts of interest.

The ethics and compliance department is responsible for creating and maintaining rules and procedures for the code of business conduct and the process by which conflicts of interest will be handled.

(17) (B) Three.

Best practices are put into place in three stages of the AHRQ process: managing staff, creating a prevention work organization and transforming operational processes to accommodate best practices.

(18) (C) Shared values, style, staff and skills.

This McKinsey 7-S Model delves into seven distinct elements, each of which affects the others. This provides change agents with a great deal of leverage when it comes to identifying loopholes in an organization's structure, processes and systems. Hard elements represent the first three elements, whereas soft elements represent the remaining elements (shared values, style, staff and skills).

(19) (B) To evaluate performance, improve quality and help organizations be efficient.

The Baldrige Criteria for Performance Excellence provides an effective method to improve efficiency and handle complex problems in the provision of medical care.

(20) (C) Standards have been audited, reviewed and approved by a qualified party.

Having ISO 9001 certification means that a company has met all the requirements of the international standardization organization. ISO standards contain written descriptions of specifications of quality, safety and efficiency applicable to multiple products, services and systems.

(21) (C) A Magnet Hospital Recognition Program for Excellence in Nursing Services.

Based on a study conducted in 1983 by the American Academy of Nursing that identified characteristics that led health-care organizations to excel in recruiting and retaining nurses, the Magnet Hospital Recognition Program for Excellence in Nursing Services was approved in December 1990 by the Board of Directors of the American Nurses Association (ANA).

(22) (C) To ensure and inspect internal operations.

An organization's internal audit and investigation department guarantees and audits compliance within the organization's internal operations. Several departments within a health-care organization have to be certified as complying with Medicare standards. Medicare compliance departments must actively cooperate with other departments in health-care organizations.

(23) (B) To allow compliance leaders to gain insight into the program's effectiveness and measure its performance.

Compliance leaders can gather feedback on compliance programs' effectiveness and measure program performance through conducting compliance effectiveness surveys. A survey of compliance effectiveness can also be used to evaluate compliance programs. Compliance officers conduct reviews, inspections and audits, and monitor activities related to compliance programs.

(24) (C) Three.

Bridges' Transition Model theory breaks down the transition into three stages, so it more accurately reflects people's emotions rather than the process. Other change models focus on the transition.

(25) (C) To represent a patient's needs, concerns and expectations to the health-care organization.

Patient representatives need to be a part of a committee since they can communicate the health-care users' needs, concerns, demands and expectations to the health-care organization. The quality improvement committee conducts regular meetings to discuss areas requiring improvement based on observations made and analysis of collected data.

(26) (C) Identifying what works well in a program and what can be improved.

The purpose of evaluating programs, practices, interventions and initiatives is to discover whether they have succeeded in meeting their objectives. An evaluation identifies what works well and what needs to be improved. Making regular evaluations of your activities can help identify places for improvement and ultimately help you accomplish your goals more efficiently. Evaluation can help identify areas for improvement.

(27) (A) A patient representative.

Quality improvement committees must include representatives from numerous areas of practice. Implementation of the proposed improvement will be felt across all of these areas. Members of this committee should also include a patient representative to inform health-care organizations about consumers' needs, desires, expectations and demands.

(28) (D) Privacy and security rules.

According to the United States Department of Health and Human Services (HHS), the Privacy Rule must be respected. HIPAA security rules set standards for protecting patients' health information. These rules combine Privacy Rule protection with critical health-related data. By enforcing privacy and security rules through civil penalties and voluntary compliance, the HHS makes sure privacy and security are protected.

(29) (D) Dealing with patients with chronic conditions.

This principle ensures that the patient gets the highest level of care from a health-care provider network. It is essential to coordinate care activities to help patients with chronic conditions. Care coordination reduces care fragmentation by reducing transition time between health-care providers. Communication between health-care providers is essential to making effective referrals.

(30)   (A) Advancing clinical practice by establishing standards of care.

Implementing clinical practice guidelines is important. A clinical practice guideline may improve clinical outcomes by establishing standards of care that are supported by reliable scientific evidence, perhaps reducing variability and improving clinical care.

(31)   (B) To improve knowledge and skills.

Continuous quality improvement requires continuous improvement in education. Quality improvement courses were designed to merge theory with application in both public and higher education. This leads to more effective knowledge and skills in the science of quality improvement.

(32)   (B) To prevent, detect and correct noncompliance.

To follow CMS standards, health-care organizations must implement Medicare compliance programs. These programs serve as guidelines for health-care organizations to assess performance and make improvements.

(33)   (D) The method by which information is distributed to the public.

Information dissemination aims to deliver knowledge and evidence-based information to a bigger audience through internal or external dissemination. Internal dissemination includes sharing internal projects/information within an organization. External dissemination involves sharing information through external channels.

(34)   (C) Nurses.

Nurses today are more autonomous than ever before. They are more likely to notice the progress that is being made in patients' recovery, and they intervene on patients' behalf almost immediately when it comes to stabilization. Nursing staff may take action without seeking permission from physicians in certain cases. For example, nurses may administer magnesium to patients with dangerously low magnesium levels without obtaining permission from doctors.

(35)   (C) A person using services to prevent and treat health problems.

Health-care utilization relates to the number of people who seek treatment and/or prevention for their health problems.

(36)   (B) STEEP quality improvement method.

STEEP is a quality improvement methodology developed by the Institute of Medicine in 1999. It consists of four essential steps: identifying the problem, implementing the change, analyzing the results and introducing the change on a larger scale.

(37)   (A) Initiate, plan, execute, monitor and conclude.

A project manager will look for errors and try to predict and prevent them as much as possible while planning, organizing and controlling project activities. There are five stages to carrying out a project: initiate, plan, execute, monitor and conclude.

(38)   (D) Reaction, learning, behavior and result.

Kirkpatrick's model evaluates and examines the effectiveness of training programs. Developed by Dr. Donald Kirkpatrick in the 1950s, it is the most widely used measure of training program effectiveness. It measures training programs at four levels: reaction, learning, behavior and result.

(39)   (C) Agency or government offices.

Getting licensure from the government is a process in which individuals are permitted to engage in a profession, provided that they satisfy the minimum level of competence needed for the public's safety. In order to be licensed, a professional must undergo a thorough examination and be credentialed by the state. Nongovernmental organizations do not offer certification.

(40)   (A) To improve health care at the molecular level.

Medical nanotechnology and nano-devices offer promising new opportunities in health care. This technology provides better health control at the molecular level. Nano pharmaceutical firms are striving for focused delivery of drugs and systems that only target tumors, not the entire body.

Health Data Analytics Answers

(41)   (D) To conduct research more efficiently.

The data collection tool is a device used to collect information, such as a paper interview form or computer-assisted interviewing software. There are various tools available, and choosing the right one helps researchers conduct their work more efficiently.

(42)   (D) It discusses people's experiences with some events.

Reactions to unusual occurrences are measured using phenomenology, so it is important to think about the whole picture, not just facts and figures. Among the examples of phenomenological research is the analysis of the traumatic experiences of people involved in natural disasters.

(43)   (A) To create value.

Organizations have started to rely on intangible assets to create value, which makes a robust data management strategy increasingly important. An organization's management of digital data involves a range of policies, procedures and practices. Besides this, data management enables people and organizations to optimize the use of data while collecting, storing, retaining and utilizing it in the most secure, efficient and cost-effective manner within the limits of policies and regulations.

(44)   (D) All of the above.

The task of data management covers a wide range of factors, such as data being created, accessed and updated across multiple data tiers; cloud storage and on-premises storage; managing disaster recovery and high availability; learning about new apps, analytics and algorithms across the web using data; ensuring the security and privacy of the data and maintaining data retention schedules and compliance requirements while archiving and destroying data.

(45)   (D) All of the above.

Health data includes different forms of information. The type of data produced within the health system depends on the patient's experience, hospital response, treatment or therapy. However, sometimes data can be specific to a disease, just like the collection of data regarding the coronavirus pandemic. Medical and public health organizations are increasingly integrating health data visualization because of the increased use of available tools.

(46)   (A) Phenomenology.

Phenomenology discusses people's experiences with some events. Among the examples of phenomenological research is the analysis of the traumatic experience of people involved in natural disasters.

(47)   (A) Qualitative method.

Qualitative data collection looks at the information in greater detail and lends a greater understanding to the raw data. This method evaluates psychological factors, such as the thoughts and feelings of patients. In this method, the type of data is in nonnumeric form; it is in the form of words (e.g., observations, descriptions).

(48)   (C) Data visualization.

Displaying or visualizing data is the process of using graphics to present information, statistics and data. Charts, graphs and maps offer a quick and clear way of reading and understanding the information or statistics. To make data-driven decisions, display tools and technologies are important to analyze massive amounts of information.

(49)   (A) They provide real-time results of what is occurring within a hospital setting.

Operational dashboards provide real-time results of what is occurring within a hospital setting. For example, they may show admission details that can be reviewed throughout the day. A strategic dashboard shows patterns and trends over time. The analytical dashboard can be used to provide data on a broader scale.

(50)   (D) All of the above.

Presenting data in effective and interesting ways can be accomplished with several visualization approaches. The kind of information being presented differs from visualization designs, as well as the audience to whom it is being presented. The most common visualization tools are charts, tables, graphs, maps, infographics and dashboards.

(51)   (C) They can be used to provide data on a broader scale.

Analytical dashboards can be used to provide data on a broader scale. One example of using an analytical dashboard is analyzing a large collection of patient medical records to find specific trends. In contrast, operational dashboards provide real-time results of what is occurring within a hospital setting. For example, they may show admission details that can be reviewed throughout the day. A strategic dashboard shows patterns and trends over time.

(52)   (D) All of the above.

Grounded theory has three methods, which are participant observation, interviews and document or artifact collection. In participant observation, the researcher studies the subjects by observing. The purpose of interviews is to gather data from the subjects on a wide variety of topics. Moreover, to interpret documents and elicit meaning, gain meaningful insight and develop empirical knowledge, the data in question must be examined and interpreted.

(53)   (A) To determine a program's success.

Various evaluation techniques are used to determine a program's success, effectiveness and efficiency by gathering information throughout its implementation.

(54)   (D) All of the above.

The assessment process should include questions, measures, approaches to assessing and processes for collecting data.

(55)   (D) All of the above.

Random sampling is the sampling method in which each observation from the population has an equal chance of being included in the study until the desired sample size is achieved. In convenience sampling, samples are taken in locations that are convenient for the sampler. In clustered sampling, the researchers use subgroups instead of individuals.

(56)   (A) Evaluation.

An evaluation can be an excellent means of communicating information so that the community will be influencing policy decisions and promoting a sense of accountability.

(57)   (B) They show patterns and trends over time.

A strategic dashboard shows patterns and trends over time. For instance, executives at a hospital can see how patient lengths of stay have changed month over month, whereas operational dashboards provide real-time results of what is occurring within a hospital setting. For example, they may show admission details that can be reviewed throughout the day. The analytical dashboard can be used to provide data on a broader scale.

(58)   (A) Anthropology defines ethnography as the study of human societies.

Ethnography is one of the most used qualitative data collection methods. Anthropology defines ethnography as the study of human societies and cultures. It helps in understanding how people live their lives. A subject's viewpoint, rather than that of the researchers, is taken. Researchers use observation to discover the reasons why patients behave in the way they do. Ethnography is a useful qualitative approach to address a particular type of research question.

(59)   (A) Statistical tools.

In today's data-driven world, quality management relies on several statistical tools for monitoring and controlling quality.

(60)　(C) Both A and B.

Data collection, analysis and root cause identification are used as quality tools for problem-solving, process improvement and performance measurement. This helps the organization in proper planning.

(61)　(C) The researchers study the subjects by observing.

In participant observation, researchers study subjects by observing. They also immerse themselves in the subjects' lives and interactions.

(62)　(D) All of the above.

Data collection is divided into two types: qualitative and quantitative. In qualitative data collection, the data is in nonnumeric form; it is in the form of words (observations and descriptions), whereas in quantitative data collection, data is measured in the form of numbers (percentages and comparisons). Several of the methods are quantitative, dealing with something that can be counted. Others are qualitative, which means there are factors other than numbers to be considered. Records, questionnaires and documents are quantitative. Interviews, observations and oral histories are qualitative.

(63)　(A) Bar graphs and line graphs.

Bar graphs and line graphs combine to create the Pareto chart. It consists of identifying the facts necessary to set priorities. It organizes and presents information in a way that becomes easy to comprehend.

(64)　(A) It looks at the information in greater detail.

Qualitative data collection looks at the information in greater detail and lends a greater understanding to the raw data. This method evaluates psychological factors, such as the thoughts and feelings of patients. This method goes beyond collecting data, whereas in quantitative data collection methods, the data is measured in the form of numbers.

(65) (C) Both A and B.

Bar graphs and line graphs combine to create the Pareto chart. Moreover, line graphs represent the percentage of defects for a specific period.

(66) (D) Its purpose is to gather data from the subjects on a wide variety of topics.

The purpose of interviews is to gather data from the subjects on a wide variety of topics. The interviews can be formal or informal.

(67) (A) Data collection tools.

Primary data collection in organizations can be carried out using several tools. These methods include traditional and straightforward approaches to data collection and analysis, such as face-to-face interviews, as well as more advanced approaches, such as data mining.

(68) (D) All of the above.

The three most-used qualitative data collection methods are ethnography, grounded theory and phenomenology. Anthropology defines ethnography as the study of human societies and cultures. It helps in understanding how people live their lives. The grounded theory is used to explore social interactions within human relationships. The study of phenomenology discusses people's experiences with some events or encounters. Reactions to unusual occurrences are measured using this method.

(69) (D) None of the above.

To interpret documents and elicit meaning, gain meaningful insight and develop empirical knowledge, the data in question must be examined and interpreted. Materials used by a group can provide researchers with valuable information.

(70) (D) It enables large companies to collect tiers of data efficiently.

A data management platform enables large companies to easily and efficiently collect and analyze tiers of data, utilizing existing or new tools developed by a software vendor or a third party.

(71)   (B) Data measured in the form of numbers.

In qualitative data collection, the data is in non-numeric form (observations and descriptions).

(72)   (A) Administrative and financial data.

In health-care management, health-care data analysis provides a combination of financial and administrative data, as well as information that can help improve patient care and services. Moreover, with the help of health data measurement and analysis, providers can deliver quality care using data-driven methods; optimize scheduling and staffing processes to minimize patient wait times; streamline processes related to making appointments, processing insurance, and providing referrals and improve patient experience by providing more personalized treatment.

(73)   (C) It is used to explore social interactions within human relationships.

Grounded theory has been an influential force in the qualitative methods in various areas of social science application. This theory is used to explore social interactions within human relationships.

(74)   (D) Using graphics to present information.

Displaying or visualizing data is the process of using graphics to present information, statistics, and data. Charts, graphs and map displays offer a quick and clear way of reading and understanding the information or statistics. To make data-driven decisions, display tools and technologies are important for analyzing massive amounts of information.

(75)   (A) Capturing useful evidence.

Data collection was designed to capture useful evidence that will facilitate analysis, which will lead to the formulation of convincing and credible answers to the questions posed.

Performance and Process Improvement Answers

(76)   (B) Six Sigma.

Six Sigma is a management tool used to enhance patient safety and quality of health care. It provides 99.99966 percent productivity without defects.

(77)   (A) It is a crucial capability for constructing a more effective and patient-oriented health-care delivery system.

The number of team members does not guarantee teamwork. A lot of team members can turn out to be less skilled, less contributing and a burden on the team.

(78)   (B) PDCA.

PDCA, or Plan-Do-Check-Act, was introduced by Walter Shewhart in 1929. It was made popular by W. Edwards Deming in the 1950s as a learning method.

(79)   (D) 40%.

Teamwork is essential in all fields of life. In health care, it is extremely important because it reduces medical errors by 40 percent. Medical errors are the third-leading cause of death in the United States. If the medical errors are reduced, the number of deaths will also decrease.

(80)   (C) Staff members working together.

The number of staff members does not matter. If the staff is working together, it will encourage the physicians to get involved in health care with more dedication.

(81)   (D) None of the above.

All the groups in hospitals that are responsible for providing direct care to patients are a part of the core team. They include doctors, pharmacists, nurses and case managers.

(82)   (C) Both A and B.

The coordinating team in a health-care setting involves the groups responsible for ensuring coordination between the systems and managing their operations.

(83)   (A) Six Sigma.

DMAIC stands for Define, Measure, Analyze, Improve and Control. These five processes are used in Six Sigma, which is a management tool used to enhance patient safety and improve health-care facilities.

(84)   (B) Define.

Out of all the options provided, only Define is part of the DMAIC abbreviation.

(85)   (C) Success.

If you are assessing the success of your health-care improvement programs, financial results should be your primary consideration.

(86)   (C) Support services group.

For a health-care facility, a support services group provides relational, logistical and administrative support.

(87)   (A) Ishikawa diagrams.

Fishbone diagrams are also known as Ishikawa diagrams. These diagrams are a graphical representation of the causes of an effect. They help in identifying the areas and sectors of the hospital that require improvement.

(88)   (D) Health Foundation.

This definition of health care was issued officially by the Health Foundation.

(89)   (B) The patient's electronic health records.

EHRs are the only reliable source of obtaining information about a patient's medical history.

(90)   (A) Healthcare Failure Mode and Effect Analysis.

HFMEA stands for Healthcare Failure Mode and Effect Analysis, an analysis carried out before the launch of a system. It identifies the failure modes in a system and the consequences. Those failure modes are then fixed, and the efficiency of a system is increased.

(91)   (A) Patient-centered.

To see visible improvements in the quality of health care you provide, you must set your goals on the six pillars of health care: safe, effective, patient-centered, equitable, timely and efficient.

(92)   (B) By designing a mechanism that allows for equitable distribution of health-care facilities across the board.

Cutting off these groups will further aggravate the disparities. Increasing the number of staff members belonging to these groups will also not help. You must devise a plan that enables the equitable distribution of health care to people, irrespective of their background.

(93)   (D) Root cause analysis.

After a system is launched and a problem is observed, root cause analysis allows you to explore the causes of the problem and fix it so that the system works better the next time.

(94)   (D) Both A and B.

To create an effective team, variations are incredibly important. People from different backgrounds, with different sets of skills, should be made a part of the team.

(95)   (C) The service volumes needed to ensure safe and effective care.

The other options are not correct because the importance of clinical education refers to academic commitments, and the community's clinical requirements are called the community needs.

(96)   (A) W. Edwards Deming.

PDCA was proposed for the first time by Walter Shewhart in 1929. It was made popular by W. Edwards Deming as a learning model in the 1950s.

(97)   (C) Assessment of current procedure.

In the planning stage of PDCA, the current procedures are assessed so that loopholes are identified for future corrections.

(98)   (B) An employee who is dedicated to improving a specific sector of the health-care setting.

A person devoted to bringing positive changes in a particular sector of a health-care setting is considered a champion. This can be a doctor, pharmacist, nurse, etc.

(99)   (C) Process map.

This map illustrates a shrunken summary of all the processes running in your health-care systems.

(100)   (A) Work breakdown structure.

WBS, or work breakdown structure, is a mechanism that allows you to divide the tasks into several different parts, where each part is assigned to a separate department, and decentralized decisions and conclusions are made.

(101)   (C) Activities.

A precedence diagram method provides illustrations with the help of nodes and arrows. Nodes signify the activities, and arrows signify the internal relationships between those activities.

(102)   (A) The goal.

As the name suggests, reverse planning starts from the end. When you opt for reverse planning, you first determine the goal and then the procedure to achieve that goal.

(103)   (A) Management with attention to minor details.

The word *micro* means "small." Hence micromanagement is management in which attention is given to every minor detail.

(104)   (B) Patient experience, health and cost.

In health care, the three aims of the Triple Aim are patient experience, health and cost.

(105)   (D) Both B and C.

Comments and observations provide more information about an individual than numeric ratings do. This is because, in numeric ratings, only a value is assigned. However, in comments and observations, a lot more detail is mentioned.

(106)   (D) All of the above.

Structure attributes of a health-care organization include bed capacity, availability of health insurance and training of nurses. When you measure the structure attributes, you need to consider all three of these.

(107) (A) Root cause analysis.

RCA stands for root cause analysis. It is a technique that is used when a problem is identified after the launch of a system.

(108) (C) Fishbone diagrams.

Fishbone diagrams, also known as Ishikawa diagrams, are graphical representations of the causes of an effect. They enable a team to identify the regions or sectors of a hospital that require improvements.

(109) (C) Both A and B.

To make the quality of health care better, you must control your processes so that they ensure better future performance and provide greater improvements.

(110) (B) Detailed documents.

Word of mouth can never provide complete and detailed information. A process map is a summarized version of all the processes being run. The detailed documents about processes can be fruitful in such a scenario.

(111) (B) Hierarchical approach.

The hierarchical approach is applied to gather the resources available in the system.

(112) (A) Determining the performance of resources.

Resource estimating refers to determining the performance of the resources that are part of a system.

(113)   (B) Nonlinear.

Reverse planning is a nonlinear process.

(114)   (C) Eight.

A questionnaire is designed to assess the team. There are eight dimensions of this questionnaire: purpose and goals, underlying team relationships, problem-solving ability, roles, team process, intergroup relationships, passion and commitment, and skills and learning.

(115)   (A) IHI.

IHI, the Institute of Healthcare Improvement, suggests that forming a balanced team is a key and primary step in attaining improvements in health-care facilities.

Patient Safety Answers

(116)   (B) Root cause analysis.

It is the analysis of the root causes behind the occurrence of a problem in health care.

(117)   (D) Prioritizes patient safety.

The only organization worth your time and attention is the one that prioritizes the safety of patients.

(118)   (A) An event that causes harm to a patient.

An adverse event is best described as an event that inflicts an injury or damage to a patient, harming his or her safety.

(119)   (D) Patient safety.

This is the definition of patient safety issued by the World Health Organization. Patient safety refers to the absence of adverse events and ensures the provision of the best medical care.

(120)   (A) American Medical Association.

This is the definition of patient safety issued by the American Medical Association (AMA).

(121)   (B) Intensive care unit.

The intensive care unit is a department in a hospital that provides critical care and life support to extremely ill patients.

(122)   (A) A system that functions independently from a network.

As the name suggests, a stand-alone system works on its own, separately from a network. This makes the system incredibly secure.

(123)   (B) Medical errors.

According to a Johns Hopkins study, after heart diseases and cancer, medical errors contribute the most to deaths every year in the United States.

(124)   (B) Immediately remove the patient from the ICU with an oxygen supply.

If a patient is on a ventilator, the individual cannot breathe on his/her own. Therefore, it is important to first evacuate the person to a safer place before even extinguishing the fire.

(125)   (C) Resolved domestic issues.

A patient safety program can only ensure a reduction in falls and better medication. It cannot be held responsible if any domestic issues occur after a patient is discharged from the hospital.

(126)   (D) Both B and C.

Depression is a mental illness that is not caused by poor patient safety. However, falls and medical errors are both a result of poor patient safety in a hospital.

(127)   (D) All of the above.

Administration of medicine, diagnosis of a disease and usage of equipment are all different procedures. Thus, all the options provided can be classified as errors.

(128)   (A) Root cause analysis.

Failure mode and effect analysis is conducted before the launch or start of a system where potential failure points are identified and corrected. Root cause analysis is performed after a problem has occurred. It identifies the root causes of the problem so that it can be avoided the next time.

(129) (C) Electronic health record systems.

Electronic health record systems produce paperless, patient-centric records that are up to date and easy to carry.

(130) (A) Power breakdown.

Power breakdown, wrong equipment usage and the use of malfunctioning equipment all lead to equipment failure. However, the hospital cannot be held responsible for a power breakdown because it is usually unpredictable and unexpected. Any problem arising due to a power breakdown can be solved only after the power breakdown has occurred.

(131) (B) EHR systems help speed up physicians' diagnosing process.

An electronic health record system helps speed up the diagnosing process.

(132) (C) A near-miss.

A near miss is an event that has the potential of causing damage but doesn't.

(133) (A) Risk assessments.

Installation of an embedded system does not help in minimizing risks. Root cause analysis is done after a problem has occurred; an overview refers to skimming through the situation. On the other hand, risk assessments are conducted before the launch or initiation of a problem to identify the risks beforehand and resolve them.

(134) (D) All of the above.

If a patient's safety is compromised in a hospital, all the people working in it can be held responsible.

(135)   (B) A nurse selects the drug and its concentration from the list in the system of the pumps, and the medication is then infused into the patient.

These pumps are not self-operating. A nurse has to select the drug along with its dose first.

(136)   (A) Global trigger tool.

A global trigger tool helps easily identify adverse events, which can otherwise take long hours of extensive analysis.

(137)   (C) Review.

Education and training are mediums of transferring information and knowledge from one person to another. To overview means to skim through a situation, which is a review that investigates, analyzes, responds and reports functions of the incident.

(138)   (B) Systems thinking.

Systems thinking is an approach that allows you to have an in-depth view of the system and all of its components. This approach enables you to rectify issues in the system and resolve them.

(139)   (A) By providing information regarding patient safety and adverse events to all patients.

If you keep patients updated about their health, the steps regarding patient safety and any adverse events, they will feel more comfortable opening up to you.

(140)   (B) It is a component of a device or an application that allows humans to engage with machines.

Human-machine interface is where humans and machines meet or engage.

Test 3

Organizational Leadership Questions

(1)   What are best practices?

(A)   Tactics to better help patients in a health-care organization

(B)   Development of nurses in health-care organizations

(C)   Strategies employed by high-performing health-care organizations

(D)   Tactics that are used to develop strategies for better health-care workers

(2)   Who educates patients on medication intake?

(A)   Paramedics

(B)   Nurses

(C)   Doctors

(D)   Surgeons

(3)   What can be ensured if best practices are implemented?

(A)   Patient satisfaction

(B)   An improved image for the organization

(C)   Safety of patients' personal information

(D)   Practitioners and staff performing at their best, both effectively and efficiently

(4)   How many times does the quality improvement committee gather to propose improvements based on data collected and identify areas with room for improvement?

(A)   Once every week

(B)   Once a year

(C)   On a regular basis

(D)   Once a month

(5)   What is one pillar of nursing?

(A)   Advocacy

(B)   Efficiency

(C)   Intellect

(D)   Diligence

(6)   How do external best practices help managers?

(A)   They provide training programs to doctors.

(B)   They help with marketing effectively.

(C)   They reduce medical errors.

(D)   They identify gaps and find productive ways to fill them.

(7)   What is the very first step toward quality improvement?

(A)   Being objective

(B)   Collecting data

(C)   Careful planning

(D)   Time management

(8)   According to the WHO, what helps people take more control over their health?

(A)   Introduction of new treatment methods

(B)   Advancements in technology

(C)   Health promotion

(D)   Introduction of new medications

(9)   What type of culture does the deployment of external best practices provide to organizations?

(A)   A culture that promotes old tactics

(B)   A culture that promotes innovative and creative ideas

(C)   A culture that promotes utilizing fewer resources

(D)   A culture that promotes less experimentation

(10)   Who helps patients when they are hesitant to ask the right questions?

(A)   Paramedics

(B)   Doctors

(C)   Advocates

(D)   Nurses

(11)   What is an episode of care?

(A)   An entire treatment based on a doctor's advice

(B)   An entire treatment based on health promotion

(C)   An entire treatment based on modern methods

(D)   An entire treatment based on class or category

(12)   What is the first step for implementing change in an organization?

(A)   Introduce new HR tactics

(B)   Analyze current systems and processes

(C)   Introduce new technologies

(D)   Train staff

(13)   What does health-care utilization measure?

(A)   Efficiency of the treatments provided by doctors

(B)   Effectiveness of new medications

(C)   Resources utilized in treatments

(D)   Services utilized by a person to prevent and treat health problems

(14)   What type of organization is the Joint Commission?

(A)   Hierarchical structure

(B)   Accrediting and standard-setting

(C)   Divisional

(D)   Functional

(15)   What are the components that help identify areas that require improvement in a health-care organization?

(A)   Managing and allocating

(B)   Organizing and controlling

(C)   Planning and executing

(D)   Monitoring and auditing

(16)   What type of requirements do health organizations need to comply with in order to avoid being fined or faced with penalties?

(A)   External and internal requirements

(B)   Quality standard requirements

(C)   Statutory and regulatory requirements

(D)   Regional and cultural requirements

(17)   What type of compliance focuses on the requirements imposed or enforced by a federal agency or state?

(A)   Internal compliance

(B)   Regulatory compliance

(C)   External compliance

(D)   Statutory compliance

(18)   Which change model can be deployed in simple or complex health-care organizations?

(A)   The McKinsey 7-S Model

(B)   The ADKAR change management model

(C)   The nudge theory change model

(D)   Lewin's change model

(19)   What is the purpose of reinforcement in the ADKAR change model?

(A)   To make drastic changes

(B)   To make no changes

(C)   To make sustainable changes

(D)   To make effective changes

(20)   What are the five goals for patient care and safety in the STEEP quality improvement method?

(A)   Evaluation, analysis, demonstration, purpose, objective and goals

(B)   Safety, timeliness, effectiveness, efficiency and patient-centeredness

(C)   Aim, target, plan, requirements, commitment and passion

(D)   Dedication, application, innovation, concentration, effort and persistence

(21)   Where are the assessments made by nurses kept?

(A)   Patients' personal information

(B)   Patients' diagnostic information

(C)   Patients' medical records

(D)   Patients' financial records

(22)　What type of organization does Det Norske Veritas (DNV) require report any adverse events?

(A)　Certified organization

(B)　Affiliated organization

(C)　Licensed organization

(D)　Accredited organization

(23)　Which institutions are the biggest stakeholders in the health-care sector?

(A)　Private institutions

(B)　Government institutions

(C)　Social institutions

(D)　Political institutions

(24)　What is an efficient and effective means of communication?

(A)　Health communication technology

(B)　Meeting management

(C)　Patient-provider-family caregiver interactions

(D)　Health Promotion

(25)   What department deals with the detection, correction and prevention of external fraud?

(A)   Human resources

(B)   Patient treatment investigation

(C)   Security and privacy

(D)   External audit and investigation

(26)   What do internal requirements work to fight?

(A)   Corrupting elements a corporation may encounter

(B)   Introduction of new medications

(C)   Introduction of new technology

(D)   Number of errors made

(27)   What is the purpose of the HIPAA privacy and security rules?

(A)   Protect patients' personal information

(B)   Protect patients' diagnostic information

(C)   Protect patients' medical history

(D)   Protect patients' critical health information

(28)   Misdiagnosis is the result of what?

(A)   Poor management of staff

(B)   Poor training provided to doctors

(C)   Poor-quality health-care services

(D)   Poor implementation of strategies

(29)   What tool is used to determine whether a program is ready for accreditation?

(A)   Certification test

(B)   Accreditation Readiness Self-Assessment

(C)   Licensing

(D)   Affiliated marketing

(30)   What services does CARF provide?

(A)   National and international accreditation services

(B)   National and international certificate services

(C)   National and international regulation services

(D)   National and international affiliation services

(31)   What process can help organizations find areas of improvement?

(A)   Analysis

(B)   Evaluation

(C)   Inspection

(D)   Assessment

(32)   What is the first stage of implementing best practices according to the Agency for Healthcare Research and Quality?

(A)   Training staff

(B)   Managing staff

(C)   Introducing new treatment methods

(D)   Making technological advancements in medical equipment

(33)   What are the seven elements the McKinsey 7-S Model is divided into?

(A)   Horizontal and vertical elements

(B)   Hard and soft elements

(C)   Internal and external elements

(D)   Statutory and regulatory elements

(34)   What is precision medicine used for?

(A)   To increase the effectiveness of the medicine

(B)   To reduce the risks of any unwanted reaction

(C)   To reduce the treatment time

(D)   To reduce the quantity of medicine intake

(35)   What health promotion activity transfers the patient's information, responsibility and authority from one health-care provider to another?

(A)   Health-care utilization

(B)   Handoff activity

(C)   Transition of care

(D)   Episode of care

(36)   What is the method by which facts or information are distributed to the public?

(A)   Information processing

(B)   Legal analysis

(C)   Information dissemination

(D)   Communication strategies

(37)   What program is implemented in order to drive employee engagement, reduce voluntary nursing staff turnover and increase employee loyalty?

(A)   Recognition program

(B)   Identification program

(C)   Awareness program

(D)   Marketing program

(38) Who does the quality improvement committee report?

(A)   Managers of the organization

(B)   CEO of the organization

(C)   Staff of the organization

(D)   Owner of the organization

(39)   To enter fields like EKG and cardio-phlebotomy tech, what is required?

(A)   A license

(B)   Affiliation

(C)   Certification

(D)   Accreditation

(40)   A health-care professional's desired level of performance should be based on:

(A)   Doctor performance

(B)   Duration of treatment

(C)   Behavior of staff

(D)   Patients' expectations

Health Data Analytics Questions

(41)   Which of the following statements is true about quantitative observation?

(A)   It is more accurate than qualitative observation.

(B)   There are five primary quantitative research methods.

(C)   Interviews, observations and oral histories are qualitative.

(D)   All of the above.

(42)   A selection of measures should be made because of which of the following reasons?

(A)   To address health priorities

(B)   To deliver quality care using data-driven methods

(C)   To optimize staffing processes to minimize patient wait times

(D)   To streamline processes related to making appointments

(43)   Which of the following statements is true about a run chart?

(A)   It is a line graph that shows data points as they change over time.

(B)   It visualizes process performance and shows whether it is within acceptable limits.

(C)   It is used to evaluate the correlation between two variables.

(D)   None of the above.

(44)   To which of the following statements does a descriptive statistic refer?

(A)   It describes the characteristics of a study's data by providing simple summaries about the samples or measures.

(B)   It describes what the data shows rather than analyzing it directly.

(C)   Both A and B.

(D)   None of the above.

(45)   Which of the following statements refers to the descriptive research method?

(A)   It describes the current status of the variable.

(B)   It is a way to assess the relationship between two quantitative variables.

(C)   It employs the scientific method to gather information regarding cause-and-effect relationships in the environment.

(D)   None of the above.

(46)   Which of the following is a mathematical average?

(A)   Mean

(B)   Median

(C)   Correlation

(D)   T-test

(47) Which of the following is the main type of qualitative data?

(A) Nominal

(B) Ordinal

(C) Both A and B

(D) None of the above

(48) Quantitative data is divided into how many major categories?

(A) Two

(B) Three

(C) Four

(D) Six

(49) Which of the following is also known as categorical data?

(A) Qualitative data

(B) Quantitative data

(C) Numeric data

(D) None of the above

(50)   Which of the following statements correctly defines the correlational research method?

(A)   It describes the current status of the variable.

(B)   It is a way to assess the relationship between two quantitative variables.

(C)   It employs the scientific method to gather information regarding cause-and-effect relationships in the environment.

(D)   None of the above.

(51)   Which of the following data should be included in the continuous data type?

(A)   Interval

(B)   Ratio

(C)   Both A and B

(D)   None of the above

(52)   Which of the following is a branch of statistics?

(A)   Descriptive statistics

(B)   Inferential statistics

(C)   Both A and B

(D)   None of the above

(53)   Which of the following is the branch of knowledge about gathering information from data?

(A)   Statistics

(B)   Control

(C)   Process

(D)   T-test

(54)   Which of the following statements is true about a scatter diagram?

(A)   It is a line graph that shows data points as they change over time.

(B)   It visualizes process performance and shows whether it is within acceptable limits.

(C)   It is used to evaluate the correlation between two variables.

(D)   None of the above.

(55)   To which of the following categories do maps belong?

(A)   Visualization tools

(B)   Management tools

(C)   Both A and B

(D)   None of the above

(56)   Which of the following statements correctly defines standard deviation?

(A)   It is a useful tool for describing a subject's position without saying what caused the event in the first place.

(B)   It is used for testing an assumption of a population with the help of a hypothesis.

(C)   It is a mathematical average.

(D)   None of the above.

(57)   Statistical process control is a method used for:

(A)   Measuring processes

(B)   Data analysis

(C)   Data measurement

(D)   None of the above

(58)   Data collection is divided into how many types?

(A)   Two

(B)   Three

(C)   Four

(D)   Five

(59)   How many primary quantitative research methods are there?

(A)   Two

(B)   Three

(C)   Four

(D)   Five

(60)   Which of the following statements defines the experimental research method?

(A)   It describes the current status of the variable.

(B)   It is a way to assess the relationship between two quantitative variables.

(C)   It employs the scientific method to gather information regarding cause-and-effect relationships in the environment.

(D)   None of the above.

(61)   How many relevant external data types are there?

(A)   Two

(B)   Three

(C)   Five

(D)   Four

(62)   What does managing input data include?

(A)   Storing

(B)   Classifying

(C)   Updating

(D)   All of the above

(63) Which of the following statements accurately describes correlation?

(A) It is a useful tool for describing a subject's position without saying what caused the event in the first place.

(B) It is used for testing an assumption of a population with the help of hypothesis testing.

(C) It is a mathematical average.

(D) None of the above.

(64) Which of the following statements is true about patient safety indicators?

(A) They are designed to improve patient care.

(B) They provide insight into potentially avoidable safety events that represent opportunities for improving health-care delivery.

(C) They are used to measure the clinical quality performance of a health plan.

(D) None of the above.

(65) Which of the following statements is true about a core measure?

(A) It is used to streamline processes related to making appointments.

(B) It is a nationally standardized system designed to improve patient care.

(C) It is used to deliver quality care using data-driven methods.

(D) It is used to optimize staffing processes.

(66)   Which of the following statements accurately describes the quantitative data interpretation method?

(A)   It is used to analyze categorical data.

(B)   It is usually used to analyze numerical data.

(C)   Both A and B.

(D)   None of the above.

(67)   What does the term external data refer to?

(A)   Any data that is being captured, processed and disseminated via sources outside the company

(B)   The current status of the variable

(C)   Both A and B

(D)   None of the above

(68)   Which of the following correctly defines the qualitative data interpretation method?

(A)   It is used to analyze and understand qualitative data.

(B)   It is used to analyze numerical data.

(C)   It is used to optimize staffing processes.

(D)   None of the above.

(69)   Which of the following statements is true about scorecards?

(A)   They are a tool that outlines an organization's objectives concerning strategy.

(B)   The organization's performance is measured through both dashboards and scorecards.

(C)   Both A and B.

(D)   None of the above.

(70)   Which of the following statements correctly defines mean?

(A)   It is a useful tool for describing a subject's position without saying what caused the event in the first place.

(B)   It is used for testing an assumption of a population with the help of hypothesis testing.

(C)   It is a mathematical average.

(D)   It is intended to illustrate how two variables of different types are linearly related.

(71)   What does trend analysis do?

(A)   It is used to examine past trends.

(B)   It is used to predict future movements based on trends.

(C)   Both A and B.

(D)   None of the above.

(72)   What do statistics involve?

(A)   Data collection

(B)   Data description

(C)   Data analysis

(D)   All of the above

(73)   What does validation of data refer to?

(A)   It is a decision-making process resulting in either a valid or invalid set of data.

(B)   It involves an organization maintaining records on a physical asset, such as data.

(C)   Both A and B.

(D)   None of the above.

(74)   Which of the following statements is true about dashboards?

(A)   You can visualize large sets of information with a dashboard.

(B)   They are a business intelligence tool used by most companies.

(C)   Both A and B.

(D)   None of the above.

(75)   Which of the following statements is true about a control chart?

(A)   It is a line graph that shows data points as they change over time.

(B)   It visualizes process performance and shows whether it is within acceptable limits.

(C)   It is used to evaluate the correlation between two variables.

(D)   None of the above.

Performance and Process Improvement Questions

(76) _____ reduces the medical errors in health care by 40 percent.

(A)   Better equipment

(B)   Teamwork

(C)   A lower number of nurses

(D)   Electronic health record system(s)

(77)   What does team effectiveness assessment identify?

(A)   General issues with the team

(B)   Individual performances of team members

(C)   Number of team members

(D)   None of the above

(78)   Contingency teams are assigned the role of _____ in health care.

(A)   Managing administrative issues

(B)   Managing emergency situations

(C)   Both A and B

(D)   None of the above

(79) A/An_____ functions on its own and provides support to the core team in a health-care setting.

(A)   Contingency team

(B)   Coordinating team

(C)   Ancillary team

(D)   Support services group

(80)   Avedis Donabedian is famous for proposing which of the following concepts?

(A)   Quality in health care

(B)   Speed of light

(C)   Six Sigma

(D)   Precedence diagrams

(81)   Who is responsible for a patient's care in a hospital?

(A)   Only doctors

(B)   Relatives

(C)   The entire hospital staff

(D)   Only nurses

(82) Health insurance, advanced training of nurses and the capacity of hospital beds are measured under _____.

(A) Structure attributes

(B) Quality

(C) Patient safety

(D) None of the above

(83) Which of the following are involved in the total quality management model?

(A) Transformational change

(B) Decision-making processes

(C) Team-based processes

(D) All of the above

(84) What does PDSA stand for in health-care improvement initiatives?

(A) Plan-Do-Study-Act

(B) Platelets Disorder Support Association

(C) Both A and B

(D) None of the above

(85) What do the arrows in the precedence diagram imply?

(A) The number of activities

(B) Internal relationship between activities

(C) External relationship between activities

(D) Duration of activities

(86)   Which of the following is the definition of health care issued by the Health Foundation?

(A)   Quality of facilities

(B)   Multidimensional standard of excellence

(C)   Safety from medical errors

(D)   None of the above

(87)   "Several approaches are necessary to deliver sustained health-care quality improvements." Which of the following organizations issued this statement?

(A)   WHO

(B)   IHI

(C)   HI

(D)   HF

(88)   A hospital wants to introduce an improvement initiative program. What analysis should the organization use to ensure maximum efficiency?

(A)   Root cause analysis

(B)   Total quality analysis

(C)   Six Sigma analysis

(D)   Failure mode and effect analysis

(89)   Identify the number of pillars for quality health-care improvement goals are based on.

(A)   Five

(B)   Six

(C)   None

(D)   One

(90)   Which of the following people should not be a part of a balanced team?

(A)   A senior leader

(B)   An expert clinical decision-maker

(C)   A team leader

(D)   None of the above

(91) Prospective job candidates must fit into the _____ of an organization.

(A)   Visions

(B)   Values

(C)   Goals

(D)   All of the above

(92)   Why is clinical education important in health care?

(A)   To educate future health-care professionals

(B)   To recruit and train current medical professionals

(C)   Both A and B

(D)   None of the above

(93)   In community health-based services, community needs refer to the requirements of patients _____ of the organization.

(A)   Within the local catchment area

(B)   Outside the local catchment area

(C)   Both A and B

(D)   None of the above

(94)   Which of the following best describes action planning?

(A)   Developing strategies to achieve needs

(B)   Determining needs

(C)   Getting clarity about goals

(D)   All of the above

(95)   Lean is a set of _____.

(A)   Operating philosophies

(B)   Operating methods

(C)   Operating errors

(D)   Both A and B

(96)   When did Walter Shewhart first propose PDCA?

(A)   1950

(B)   1929

(C)   1800

(D)   1345

(97)   Which of the following is a requirement of the Do stage of PDCA?

(A)   Put the plans in motion

(B)   Evaluate the information

(C)   Assess the current procedures

(D)   Make changes in the documents

(98)   What is the Six Sigma process used for?

(A)   Enhancing patient safety

(B)   Enhancing the quality of health care

(C)   Both A and B

(D)   None of the above

(99)   Which of the following reveals analytical opportunities during failure mode and effect analysis?

(A)   Error reports

(B)   Customer complaints

(C)   A near-miss event

(D)   All of the above

(100) A _____ can be used to illustrate the sequence of processes in a large health-care project.

(A) Bar graph

(B) Precedence diagram

(C) Fishbone diagram

(D) Process map

(101) Which of the following comprises a failure mode?

(A) A mishap during the completion of a process step

(B) A failed system

(C) The chances of failure in a system

(D) The ratio of success to failure of a system

(102) What happens if a failure mode occurs just before a patient intervention?

(A) Nothing happens.

(B) The patient gets injured.

(C) More harm is likely to occur to the patient.

(D) Less harm is likely to occur to the patient.

(103) Which of the following can be optimized if unnecessary and ineffective care is removed from a health-care setting?

(A)   Patient pathways

(B)   Efficiency

(C)   Efficacy

(D)   All of the above

(104) Which of the following is maintained through reverse planning?

(A)   Scope

(B)   Time

(C)   Number of patients

(D)   Both A and B

(105) What does PDM stands for in health-care improvement initiatives?

(A)   Primary democratic movement

(B)   Precedence diagram method

(C)   Public debt management

(D)   Psychodynamic diagnostic manual

(106) Which of the following is the result of advanced team training?

(A)   Increase in team effectiveness

(B)   Improvement in patient outcomes

(C)   Both A and B

(D)   None of the above

(107) Patient experience, health and cost are the three aims of _____.

(A)   RCA

(B)   Total quality management

(C)   Triple Aim

(D)   FMEA

(108) How can you instill confidence in individuals and make future improvements feasible?

(A)   Through good documentation

(B)   By increasing the number of experienced staff members

(C)   Through motivational speeches

(D)   By conducting long, frequent meetings

(109) Which of the following institutes uses PDSA as its improvement method?

(A)   Healthcare Foundation

(B)   Institute of Healthcare Improvement

(C)   World Health Organization

(D)   National Institute of Health

(110) How many processes are involved in the DMAIC methodology?

(A)   Four

(B)   Six

(C)   Five

(D)   Ten

(111) Identify another name for backward planning.

(A)   Reverse planning

(B)   Forward planning

(C)   Bottom-to-top planning

(D)   All of the above

(112) Which of the following is not part of the questionnaire designed to assess teams?

(A)   Number of team members

(B)   Roles of team members

(C)   Underlying team relationships

(D)   Intergroup relationships

(113) General and specific ratings of an employee in health care provide the organization with _____ information.

(A)   Quantitative

(B)   Qualitative

(C)   Conceptual

(D)   Empirical

(114) What should be the priority after a team effectiveness assessment is completed?

(A)   Enhancing important team member skills

(B)   Testing team members' memories

(C)   Reward the most efficient team members

(D)   None of the above

(115) What does an Ishikawa diagram illustrate?

(A)   The recovery rate of patients

(B)   The causes of an effect

(C)   The processes

(D)   None of the above

Patient Safety Questions

(116) What does WHO stand for in health care?

(A) World Health Organization

(B) White House Office

(C) Wellness Higher Operator

(D) None of the above

(117) What does patient safety refer to?

(A) Performance of the staff

(B) Protection from natural disasters

(C) Nursing care plan

(D) Preventing harm to patients and ensuring improved health-care facilities

(118) Which of the following best describes a near-miss event?

(A) An event that causes harm to a patient

(B) An event that causes harm to nurses

(C) An event that has the potential of causing harm to a patient but fails to do so

(D) An interesting event in the hospital missed by a patient

(119) _____ accounts for most of the medical errors in health care.

(A)   Medication error

(B)   Poor use of equipment

(C)   Wrong diagnosis

(D)   Absence of nurses

(120) A nurse was assigned to move a patient from an emergency ward to a general ward via a wheelchair. Due to her negligence, the patient fell off. Which of the following best describes this event?

(A)   A near miss

(B)   An adverse event

(C)   A normal event

(D)   An expected event

(121) Which of the following is the definition of patient safety issued by the World Health Organization?

(A)   The absence of preventable harm to a patient during the process of health care and reduction of risk of unnecessary harm associated with health care to an acceptable minimum

(B)   The pursuit of methods to reduce the risk of medical errors, as well as utilizing best practices for treating patients

(C)   Both A and B

(D)   None of the above

(122) To reduce medication errors, you are introducing smart infusion pumps into your hospital. Which of the following analysis should you carry out to prevent an adverse event?

(A)   Root cause analysis

(B)   Failure mode and effect analysis

(C)   Statistical analysis

(D)   Descriptive analysis

(123) A stand-alone operating system can function independently on _____.

(A)   Computers

(B)   Cell phones

(C)   Both A and B

(D)   None of the above

(124) A nurse was administering a drug to a patient. She did not realize that she was about to overdose the patient until another nurse stepped into the room. The second nurse immediately identified the extra concentration and stopped the first nurse from administering it to the patient. This event can be classified as _____.

(A)   An adverse event

(B)   A near-miss event

(C)   A mistake

(D)   A crime

(125) Which of the following is the most effective way to curb infant kidnapping from hospitals?

(A)   WiFi-linked abduction security systems

(B)   Electronic health record systems

(C)   Management information systems

(D)   Decision support systems

(126) Which of the following is the result of equipment mishandling?

(A)   Wrong diagnosis

(B)   Patient falls

(C)   Overdose of medicine

(D)   Mental health issues

(127) If medical errors were considered a disease, they would be the _____ leading cause of death in the United States.

(A)   First

(B)   Last

(C)   Second

(D)   Third

(128) Which of the following is the last thing that needs to be considered in risk assessment and management?

(A)   Patient-specific risks

(B)   Documentation

(C)   Financial consequences

(D)   Patient safety

(129) In a NICU, all the infants admitted are on artificial oxygen supply. The nurse on duty discovers a fire in the room and rushes to seek help. The fire-extinguishing staff arrives after a while and puts out the fire. In the meantime, many infants die. Instead of rushing to seek help, which of the following should have been the nurse's response in this situation?

(A)   She should have activated the fire alarm.

(B)   She should have waited for the orders of the doctors.

(C)   She should have immediately evacuated the infants with their oxygen supplies to a safe room.

(D)   She should have extinguished the fire herself with an extinguisher.

(130) What is a human-machine interface used for?

(A)   To connect a human to a machine

(B)   To connect two humans

(C)   To connect two machines

(D)   To connect a computer to machinery being used to treat patients

(131)   Which of the following health-care aspects is assessed while evaluating patient safety activities?

(A)   The experience of the paramedical staff working in the hospital

(B)   The popularity of the hospital

(C)   Equitable distribution of health-care resources among patients

(D)   The number of patients in the hospital

(132) Which of the following is an essential metric of quality in health care?

(A)   Patient hygiene

(B)   The number of trained nurses

(C)   Equipment warranties

(D)   Patient safety

(133)   Which of the following is an identifiable feature of an exceptionally reliable health-care organization?

(A)   Failures are identified and reduced on a regular basis.

(B)   Priority is given to the number of nursing staff.

(C)   A hygienic environment is maintained for patients.

(D)   Staff members who make mistakes are fired.

(134) What does a quality framework establish in an organization?

(A) The foundation for improving the quality of health care across the organization

(B) The foundation of raising the salaries of the paramedical staff working in the hospital

(C) Both A and B

(D) None of the above

(135) What does NICU stand for?

(A) National immigration center of USA

(B) Neonatal intensive care unit

(C) National intensive care unit

(D) Nurses' incredible care unit

(136) How can real-time protection mechanisms help reduce the number of infant kidnappings?

(A) They tell you when the infant was kidnapped.

(B) They tell you when the infant was last seen near the hospital.

(C) They tell you the location of the baby in real time.

(D) They tell you the number of babies kidnapped from the hospital in a day.

(137)   What does HFE stand for in health care?

(A)   Human factor engineering

(B)   High frequency executive

(C)   Heavy fuel engine

(D)   Hidden field equations

(138) _____ enable organizations to analyze, assess and improve patient safety levels.

(A)   Patient safety programs

(B)   Health-care organizations

(C)   Training programs

(D)   None of the above

(139)   Which of the following should be the main objective in risk management and assessment of patient safety plans?

(A)   Assessing financial risks

(B)   Assessing patient-centric risks

(C)   Assessing nurse-centric risks

(D)   Assessing the performance of nurses

(140) Which of the following should be the role of leaders in a health-care organization?

(A)   Lead from the front

(B)   Train subordinates and then leave the tasks to them

(C)   Give orders

(D)   None of the above

Test 3 Answers

Organizational Leadership Answers

(1) (C) Strategies employed by high-performing health-care organizations.

Health-care organizations that use best practices are known as high performers. It is almost impossible for every health-care organization to excel in every area. By implementing best practices, it can be guaranteed that practitioners and staff will perform at their best. There are two types of best practices: internal and external.

(2) (B) Nurses.

A nurse's responsibility is to make sure that patients understand their health conditions so that they can take their medications correctly. Nurses are the first people you see when you visit a doctor. A skilled nurse knows how to talk to patients and get to know them. This helps the doctor uncover important health information about the patient.

(3) (D) Practitioners and staff performing at their best, both effectively and efficiently.

Implementing best practices can guarantee that service providers and staff are performing to their maximum potential efficiently and profitably. The best practices of a high-performing health-care organization refer to its strategies and tactics.

(4) (C) On a regular basis.

To improve health-care quality in an organization, the quality improvement committee meets on a regular basis to suggest improvements based on the observation and analysis of data collected and the identification of areas where improvements can be made. The patient representative should be included as a member of the quality improvement committee in order to share consumers' needs, wants and expectations with the health-care organization. Any proposed quality improvement should require the participation of professionals from multiple areas of practice.

(5) (A) Advocacy.

Nurses are advocates for patients during treatment. This advocacy is the cornerstone of nursing. Nurses spend the most time with patients. This insight helps nurses understand patients' concerns, wants, needs and behaviors.

(6)   (D) They identify gaps and find productive ways to fill them.

External best practices help managers devise strategies to enhance productivity and creativity in an organization. By implementing external best practices, they can identify gaps that hinder the organization's productivity, fill them and design effective processes that improve employee performance and streamline business relationships.

(7)   (C) Careful planning.

Quality improvement starts with careful planning. You must analyze the current problems and the best possible solutions. A quality improvement plan should be developed that states why your organization wants to improve, what it has to do to succeed, what results should be expected, etc.

(8)   (C) Health promotion.

In line with WHO guidelines, health promotion programs help people stay healthy by taking control of various health hazards associated with a sedentary lifestyle. Such programs also encourage adopting healthy habits and lifestyle changes to lower the risk of chronic diseases.

(9)   (B) A culture that promotes innovative and creative ideas.

Health care is affected by care disparities, health-care outcomes and culture. A culture that promotes creative thinking and innovation is created by integrating external best practices into an organization. By doing so, a higher level of productivity and greater improvement in the organization's performance is achieved.

(10)   (D) Nurses.

In addition to caring for individuals, nurses are responsible for advancing public health through innovation and change in health care and public health. They are the instigators of social change. Patients with low health literacy may have difficulty understanding information or knowing what questions to ask about their conditions and/or treatments. Nurses are there to take charge and help patients in every way possible. They ensure patients understand everything they need to know about their treatment.

(11)   (B) Entire treatment based on health promotion.

An episode of care is a process of health promotion. Promoting healthy behaviors and making lifestyle changes that prevent chronic diseases and other morbidities are goals of health promotion programs.

(12)   (B) Analyze current systems and processes.

A successful change process begins with an analysis of current systems and processes. In order to improve an area, it needs to be unfrozen on Lewin's change model. This enables everyone to understand the need for change. The change models used in health care provide a road map and help implement change by providing a framework and methods to overcome barriers. Furthermore, change models provide a way to implement change in health care that relies on a proven approach based on human behavior.

(13)   (D) Services utilized by a person to prevent and treat health problems.

Health-care utilization analyzes each patient's use of the system to identify potential health problems and treat them effectively. It also gathers and analyzes the patients' prognosis and health status.

(14)   (B) Accrediting and standard-setting.

The Joint Commission is an independent organization that accredits and sets standards for the health-care industry. Although the Joint Commission has provided standardized protocols for assessing health-care organizations' quality and safety for more than six decades, it continues to make significant improvements in its methods.

(15) (D) Monitoring and auditing.

A health-care organization's monitoring and auditing processes identify areas for improvement while simultaneously making sure the current systems work correctly. Monitoring involves detecting compliance risks inherent in an organization's operations and striving to prevent them. The audit process is systematic and objective in evaluating and improving compliance programs.

(16) (C) Statutory and regulatory requirements.

According to the legal and regulatory requirements, the Center for Medicare & Medicaid Services regulates health care in the United States. Health-care organizations must adhere to these requirements to avoid being penalized. Standards require an organization to determine how its products and services are related to any statutory or regulatory requirements. An organization must demonstrate compliance with those requirements within its quality management system.

(17) (C) External compliance.

Internal compliance takes care of requirements pertaining to company operations. External compliance focuses on compliance requirements imposed or enforced by a federal or state authority. External compliance is highly influenced by effectively managing internal processes, including control, retention, disposal, inventory, security, vendor management and training.

(18) (D) Lewin's change model.

An organization can customize Lewin's change model to fit its needs. It can be employed in simple and complex health-care organizations. Through the change phase, multiple parts can be covered that serve as a deterrent against resistance and provide needed training to employees.

(19) (C) To make sustainable changes.

Reinforcement is a part of the ADKAR change model; it is used to make sustainable changes. Reinforcement is the last element of the ADKAR model, but it must be used to build momentum as change occurs.

(20)   (B) Safety, timeliness, effectiveness, efficiency and patient-centeredness.

The five goals for patient care and safety in the STEEP quality improvement method are safety, timeliness, effectiveness, efficiency and patient-centeredness.

(21)   (C) Patients' medical records.

Nurses make assessments, summarize them and document them in the patients' permanent medical records. These documents are crucial for appropriately communicating patient information to the health-care team. Nurses are also responsible for constantly updating these records.

(22)   (D) Accredited organization.

Det Norske Veritas (DNV) obliges accredited hospitals to report adverse events.

(23)   (B) Government institutions.

Health care is primarily a state issue, but government institutions are involved in the creation of efficient health-care systems as well. But it is the responsibility of health-care organizations to communicate their problems in providing care to patients.

(24)   (B) Meeting management.

The process of meeting management refers to the process of gathering patient information, planning, organizing and achieving effective results for health-care organizations during critical times. There are times when the clinical team assembles to discuss patient reports, problems, uncertainties and solutions. Within the health-care organization, meetings are a very effective tool for communication; they also have a major role in improving efficiency. This involves the challenge of ensuring that meetings are focused, inclusive and productive.

(25)   (D) External audit and investigation.

This department works with other departments and operational areas to ensure the Medicare compliance program is effectively and consistently implemented.

(26)   (A) Corrupting elements a corporation may encounter.

Internal requirements serve primarily to achieve a corporation's goals in the fight against corruption. Companies have strict internal policies that include establishing a board of directors, conducting initial director meetings, appointing independent directors, issuing shares to shareholders and recording stock transfers.

(27)   (D) Protect patients' critical health information.

HIPAA protects patients' critical personal health-related information. The Privacy Rule's protection extends to critical health data that has been saved or transferred electronically. This includes technical and nontechnical guidelines that safeguard e-PHI.

(28)   (C) Poor-quality health-care services.

Health care under poor conditions leads to incorrect or delayed diagnosis. Diagnosis errors resulting in prolonged hospitalization and death can be prevented by maintaining quality in health care. In severe cases, misdiagnosis leads to the denial of earlier cancer treatment. Under the Civil Rights Department of HHS, the Civil Money Penalty policy and voluntary compliance provide the general rules governing privacy and security.

(29)   (B) The Accreditation Readiness Self-Assessment.

This self-assessment tool compares a program with each accreditation domain and standard laid out by the accrediting agency. It has multiple choices on each accreditation domain and standard, and it lets an organization see whether a program meets these requirements. Health-care surveys are one of the most valuable sources of health care accreditation information. Surveys offer information about a facility's cleanliness, the quality of communication and the quality of overall care delivered to patients.

(30) (A) National and international accreditation services.

CARF is an international leader in applied health and rehabilitation. It is a nonprofit group that provides international and national accreditation services upon request for health care and rehabilitation facilities and programs. Its standards are remarkably high, so services that meet them are often among the best available. The CARF certification process supports human service organizations by helping them set standards for accreditation of individuals and departments worldwide, as well as institutions and facilities.

(31) (B) Evaluation.

Regularly evaluating your activities can help you to analyze what might be lacking and ultimately help you be more effective in accomplishing your goals. Evaluation can provide you with information that can help you identify areas for improvement. The information you gather lets you evaluate your accomplishments, and in doing so, you can speak highly of your program, which is vital to maintain funding from potential and current funders.

(32) (B) Managing staff.

Within the AHRQ best practices framework, implementing best practices takes place in three phases; the first stage is managing staff, consisting of members of the team, unit-based team members and team leaders.

(33) (B) Hard and soft elements.

The McKinsey 7-S Model is deployed in those organizations that require complex changes. The elements in this model affect one another and need to be understood in order to be operationally effective. The seven elements are broken into two groups: the first three elements are known as hard elements, while the rest are referred to as soft elements. For example, strategy, structure and systems require high operating margins. Therefore, these are hard elements.

(34) (C) To reduce treatment time.

One of the benefits of precision medicine is that it reduces treatment time. This technology revolutionized treatment, diagnosis and preventive care according to the necessities and lifestyles of each patient. This is a major shift from the ordinary approach to treatment. Precision medicines are prescribed by doctors based on the results of diagnostic and genetic testing procedures.

These procedures include DNA mutation investigations, genome sequence analysis and genome rewiring. These treatments are individualized so that the patient gets the right medicine.

(35) (B) Handoff activity.

Patient information, responsibilities and authority are transferred from one health-care provider to another during a handoff.

(36) (C) Information dissemination.

Information dissemination means that facts or information are distributed to the public, whereas internal dissemination means sharing internally in your own organization. External dissemination's purpose is to spread knowledge and solid information on a larger scale. It is essential to carefully plan your dissemination efforts while considering your target audience, the message you wish to convey and the communication strategies you wish to employ.

(37) (A) Recognition program.

Many health-care organizations are increasingly focusing their reward and recognition programs on performance metrics related to quality payment programs under the Affordable Care Act to inspire employee engagement, reduce voluntary nursing staff turnover and build employee loyalty.

Most health-care administrators already know that reward programs, which motivate employees and improve patient perception of care outcomes, can increase employee motivation, so most health-care providers already have recognition programs.

(38)   (B) CEO of the organization.

It is important to establish quality improvement groups or committees in order to implement and monitor quality improvements in organizations. These groups or committees report directly to the CEO.

(39)   (C) Certification.

Health-care professionals require years of formal education. For example, the education required for surgeons, ophthalmologists and anesthesiologists exceeds 12 years. The bare minimum to enter health-care professions like EKG tech and cardio-phlebotomy tech is a certificate. Certifications usually take between 10 and 12 weeks to earn.

(40)   (D) Patients' expectations.

Implementing a patient-centered approach is vital to improving health-care processes. The performance level desired should be directly correlated with the needs and expectations of patients.

Health Data Analytics Answers

(41) (A) It is more accurate than qualitative observations.

A quantitative observation is more accurate than a qualitative observation because a numerical measurement is used.

(42) (A) To address health priorities.

A selection of measures should be made to address health priorities, such as issues related to health conditions. This measure is intended to address areas in which improvements in quality of care could have an impact on the actual and potential levels of health.

(43) (A) It is a line graph that shows data points as they change over time.

A run chart is a line graph that shows data points as they change over time. By tracking data over time, you can observe trends or patterns regarding the process.

(44) (C) Both A and B.

A descriptive statistic describes a study's data characteristics by providing simple summaries about the sample or measures. These foundations are used in every quantitative technique of data analysis, alongside simple graphics analysis.

(45) (A) It describes the current status of the variable.

Based on observational data collection, descriptive research describes the current status of the variable. It is a statistical analysis of a population sample using an approach to collect quantifiable information.

(46) (A) Mean.

Mean is a mathematical average calculated by dividing a set of values by the total number of values in a data set.

(47) (C) Both A and B.

Nominal and ordinal qualitative data are the main types of qualitative data.

(48) (A) Two.

Quantitative data is divided into two major categories: discrete and continuous data.

(49) (A) Qualitative data.

Qualitative data is also known as categorical data.

(50) (B) It is a way to assess the relationship between two quantitative variables.

Correlational research is a way to assess the relationship between two quantitative variables by evaluating how strong their correlation is. The relationship between two variables can be positive or negative, where the strongest correlation between variables carries the magnitude (+/-)1.

(51) (C) Both A and B.

Continuous data types include interval data and ratio data, all of which are numeric.

(52) (C) Both A and B.

The two main branches of statistics are descriptive statistics and inferential statistics.

(53) (A) Statistics.

Statistics is a branch of knowledge based on the gathering, summarizing, analyzing and inferring of information from data.

(54) (C) It is used to evaluate the correlation between two variables.

Scatter-plot diagrams are used to evaluate the correlation between two variables. A scatter plot displays two pairs of numerical data with one variable on each axis to examine relationships between the variables. Its uses are the validity of the cause-and-effect relationship, understanding what causes poor performance and how independent variables affect the dependent variables.

(55) (A) Visualization tools.

Maps, graphs and tables, etc., are common visualization tools.

(56) (D) None of the above.

The standard deviation of a data set is the value that represents the deviation from its mean and is calculated as the reciprocal of the variance of the data set. Each data point is calculated as the square root of variance by measuring its deviation relative to the mean.

(57) (A) Measuring processes.

Statistical process control is a method for measuring, monitoring and controlling processes.

(58) (A) Two.

Data collection is divided into two types, which are quantitative and qualitative.

(59) (B) Three.

There are three primary quantitative research methods, which are descriptive, correlational and experimental research.

(60)   (C) It employs the scientific method to gather information regarding cause-and-effect relationships in the environment.

Experimentation, also known as true experimentation, employs the scientific method to gather information regarding cause-and-effect relationships in the environment. This method makes sure that all factors that potentially influence the phenomenon of interest are controlled.

(61)   (D) Four.

There are four relevant external data types: open data, paid data, shared data and social media data.

(62)   (D) All of the above.

Managing or processing input data includes storing, classifying, updating and calculating input data.

(63)   (A) It is a useful tool for describing a subject's position without saying what caused the event in the first place.

Correlation is a statistic intended to illustrate how two variables of different types are linearly related. A simple relationship system is a useful tool for describing a subject's position without saying what caused the event in the first place.

(64)   (B) They provide insight into potentially avoidable safety events that represent opportunities for improving health-care delivery.

Patient safety indicators are measurement tools that provide insight into potentially avoidable safety events that represent opportunities for improving health-care delivery. In hospital settings, they focus specifically on problems and events that can happen after surgeries, procedures and childbirth.

(65)   (B) It is a nationally standardized system designed to improve patient care.

A core measure is a nationally standardized system designed to improve patient care. The process is designed to provide the most appropriate treatment at the right time to patients. Patients at risk for blood clots can receive preventive medications, while stroke victims can receive rehabilitation provided they have earned a grade equivalent to that of a grade I patient.

(66)   (B) It is usually used to analyze numerical data.

Quantitative data models are usually used to analyze numerical data, which is also known as quantitative data. Quantitative data is divided into two major categories: discrete and continuous. Continuous data types further include interval data and ratio data.

(67)   (A) Any data that is being captured, processed and disseminated via sources outside the company.

The term *external data* refers to any data information that is being captured, processed and disseminated via sources outside the company. External sources of finance are sources external to the business.

(68)   (A) It is used to analyze and understand qualitative data.

The qualitative data interpretation method is used to analyze and understand qualitative data, which is also known as categorical data. With this method, instead of numbers or patterns to describe data, text is used. Qualitative research consists of gathering data directly from the people who are being researched, which can be harder to analyze than quantitative research.

(69)   (C) Both A and B.

An organizational scorecard is a tool that outlines your organization's objectives concerning your strategy. Those tools are useful for firms that need to make better strategic decisions based on the measurement of performance relative to the objectives of the organization.

(70)   (C) It is a mathematical average.

Mean is a mathematical average calculated by dividing a set of values by the total number of values in a data set. It is used to estimate a population from one data set derived from a sample of the population.

(71)   (C) Both A and B.

Trend analysis is a statistical method used to examine past trends and predict future movements based on those trends. Researchers can use this method to predict future behavior based on old market data.

(72)   (D) All of the above.

Statistics involves data collection, description, analysis and inference from quantitative data as a branch of applied mathematics. The two main branches of statistics include descriptive statistics, which describes samples and populations' properties, and inferential statistics, which uses these properties to test hypotheses and draw conclusions.

(73)   (A) It is a decision-making process resulting in either a valid or invalid set of data.

Validation of data is a decision-making process resulting in either a valid or invalid set of data. General rules express the acceptable combinations of values that a decision-maker must use. Rules are applied to data; if data satisfies the rules and does not violate them, then data is deemed valid for the final use.

(74)   (C) Both A and B.

You can visualize large sets of information with a dashboard, which is a business intelligence tool used mostly by companies. Companies can evaluate their operational performance in real time since data is constantly being updated with the help of a dashboard.

(75) (B) It visualizes process performance and shows whether it is within acceptable limits.

A control chart visualizes process performance and shows whether it is within acceptable limits. You can use control charts to track a project's performance figures, like cost or schedule variance, and many other metrics.

Performance and Process Improvement Answers

(76) (B) Teamwork.

It is believed that teamwork reduces medical errors in health care by 40 percent. Medical errors are the third-leading cause of death in the United States. If medical errors are reduced, the deaths in the country will also decrease. This reflects the incredible importance of teamwork, and especially in a health-care organization.

(77) (A) General issues with the team.

A team effectiveness assessment helps you identify issues with the team and its members so that problems can then be resolved efficiently.

(78) (B) Managing emergency situations.

If an emergency arises in a hospital, the contingency team members need to take action and provide health care to critical-care patients.

(79) (C) Ancillary team.

The members of the ancillary team provide support to the core team. However, these members are not subordinates of the core team. They work on their own as a separate team.

(80) (A) Quality in health care.

Avedis Donabedian is a physician who proposed the theory of quality in health care. He suggested that the quality of health care can be gauged by assessing its structure, processes and outcomes.

(81) (C) The entire hospital staff.

Similar to patient safety, the responsibility of patient care is not on the shoulders of a single individual. The entire hospital staff, including nurses, doctors, pharmacists, etc., is responsible for ensuring the availability of quality health care for the patients.

(82) (A) Structure attributes.

Structure attributes are inherent in a particular structure. In this case, the structure is the health-care setting, and advanced training, hospital bed capacity and health insurance are some of its attributes.

(83) (D) All of the above.

Total quality management is a model that involves team-based and decision-making processes. It also involves transformational change and seeks an environment that is friendly to continuous improvements.

(84) (A) Plan-Do-Study-Act.

PDSA stands for Plan-Do-Study-Act. It is a four-step model that is used to bring positive changes and improvements in health-care initiatives.

(85) (B) Internal relationship between activities.

The precedence diagram method uses nodes and arrows to illustrate information. Nodes are used to signify activities, and arrows imply the internal relationship between those activities.

(86) (B) Multidimensional standard of excellence.

According to the Healthcare Foundation, health care is the multidimensional standard of excellence.

(87) (D) HF.

This statement is issued officially by HF, the Healthcare Foundation.

(88)   (D) Failure mode and effect analysis.

Failure mode and effect analysis, or FMEA, is an analysis carried out on systems before their launch. Through this analysis, potential failure modes are identified, along with their consequences. These failure modes are then corrected to improve the efficiency of the system before it is made available to the mainstream world.

(89)   (B) Six.

To attain visible and positive results with your health-care improvement initiatives, you must base your goals on six pillars. These pillars are safe, efficient, effective, patient-centered, equitable and timely.

(90)   (D) None of the above.

To form a balanced team in the health-care setting, you need to have a team leader, a senior leader and a critical decision-maker on board to be able to introduce efficient improvement initiatives.

(91)   (D) All of the above.

To become a part of a health-care organization, potential candidates must fit into the organization's goals, visions and values.

(92)   (C) Both A and B.

Clinical education is incredibly important in health-care settings. Only educated individuals can then go on to hire educated people and pass on knowledge to aspiring health-care professionals.

(93)   (A) Within the local catchment area.

Community needs refer to the needs of patients within the local catchment area of an organization, not outside it.

(94)   (D) All of the above.

Action planning requires you to achieve clarity about your goals and needs, then design strategies to fulfill those needs and achieve those goals.

(95)   (D) Both A and B.

Lean is a methodological technique that helps in improving patient safety and health-care facilities. It is a set of operational philosophies and methods.

(96)   (B) 1929.

PDCA, or the Plan-Do-Check-Act, was proposed by Walter Shewhart in 1929. It was later popularized in the 1950s by Edward Deming as a learning model.

(97)   (A) Put the plans in motion.

Current procedures are assessed in the Plan stage. The plans are then put in motion in the Do stage. Evaluation of information is assessed in the Check stage. Changes in documentation are made in the Act stage.

(98)   (C) Both A and B.

Six Sigma is a management tool used in health-care settings to not only improve patient safety but also ensure the availability of the best health-care facilities. This tool uses the DMAIC processes to achieve goals.

(99)   (D) All of the above.

Error reports, customer complaints and a near-miss event all provide opportunities for analysis during FMEA. Although FMEA is conducted before the launch of a system, the data obtained from different tested systems can be used for FMEA to prevent the repetition of the same mistakes.

(100)   (B) Precedence diagram.

The precedence diagram method helps in the sequencing of activities. It uses nodes and arrows for illustrations, where nodes signify the activities and arrows imply the internal relationship between those activities.

(101)   (A) A mishap during the completion of a process step.

A failure mode is a mishap during the process step of the creation of a system.

(102)   (C) More harm is likely to occur to the patient.

The patient does not get injured, but if the incident occurs just before the intervention, there is a risk of greater harm for the patient.

(103)   (D) All of the above.

When unnecessary and ineffective care is removed from the systems of a health-care setting, the efficiency and efficacy of the processes improve, improving the patient pathway.

(104)   (D) Both A and B.

Reverse planning, also known as backward planning, is a technique in which the goal is identified first. This type of planning retains time and scope.

(105)   (B) Precedence diagram method.

In health-care improvement initiatives, PDM stands for precedence diagram method. This type of diagram is a graphical representation of activities through nodes and arrows. The nodes signify the activities, and the arrows signify the internal relationship between these activities.

(106) (C) Both A and B.

When a team is provided with advanced training, it improves the collective team effectiveness and improves the health-care facilities. This consequently results in the improvement of patient outcomes.

(107) (C) Triple Aim.

Patient experience, health and cost are the three aims of Triple Aim.

(108) (A) Through good documentation.

When individuals compile good documentation, they become confident in the knowledge they have acquired. Good documentation also helps in making future improvements relatively easier.

(109) (B) Institute of Healthcare Improvement.

IHI, the Institute of Healthcare Improvement, uses the Plan-Do-Study-Act technique as its improvement model.

(110) (C) Five.

DMAIC stands for five processes: Define, Measure, Analyze, Improve and Control.

(111) (A) Reverse planning.

The other name for backward planning is reverse planning. It is a nonlinear method that starts from the end, the goal. The goal is set, then the procedure to achieve it is determined.

(112)   (A) Number of team members.

There are eight dimensions of the questionnaire that is designed to assess the teams in health-care settings. Number of team members is not part of the questionnaire.

(113)   (B) Qualitative.

General and specific ratings provide qualitative data about an individual's performance on a team in a health-care organization.

(114)   (A) Enhancing important team member skills.

After the team effectiveness assessment is completed and the team's general issues are identified, the next step is to enhance the members' skills.

(115)   (B) The causes of an effect.

Ishikawa diagrams, also called fishbone diagrams, are used to represent the causes of an effect. They help identify the areas and sectors of the hospital that require improvements.

Patient Safety Answers

(116) (A) World Health Organization.

The World Health Organization is a United Nations agency responsible for ensuring worldwide standards in international public health.

(117) (D) Preventing harm to patients and ensuring improved health-care facilities.

As the name suggests, patient safety refers to the protection of patients.

(118) (C) An event that has the potential of causing harm to a patient but fails to do so.

As the name suggests, a near-miss is an event that has the potential of causing harm to a patient but doesn't actually do so.

(119) (A) Medication error.

More than 60 percent of the medical errors in health care are caused due to negligence during medication of patients.

(120) (B) An adverse event.

An adverse event causes harm to a patient. Since in this situation a patient falls from the wheelchair, he may have experienced an injury. It is thus an adverse event.

(121) (A) The absence of preventable harm to a patient during the process of health care and reduction of risk of unnecessary harm associated with health care to an acceptable minimum.

This is the definition of patient safety officially issued by the World Health Organization.

(122) (B) Failure mode and effect analysis.

This analysis is carried out before a system is introduced or launched for the mainstream. In this analysis, potential failure points are identified, their potential consequences are identified and solutions are proposed.

(123)   (C) Both A and B.

The stand-alone operating systems can work independently from a system on both cell phones and computers.

(124)   (B) A near-miss event.

A near-miss event is an event that has the potential of causing harm to a patient but fails to do so. In this situation, if the nurse had administered the wrong dose, it would have caused harm to the patient. However, the event was avoided when another nurse intervened.

(125)   (A) WiFi-linked abduction security systems.

These highly advanced security systems provide the exact location of a baby in real time.

(126)   (B) Patient falls.

Falls occur when wheelchairs or stretchers are mishandled.

(127)   (D) Third.

Heart disease and cancer are the first- and second-leading causes of death in the United States. Medical errors are the third leading cause.

(128)   (C) Financial consequences.

Risk management plans are put in place to ensure better patient safety. They need to consider patient-specific risks. Any financial constraint is the last thing to be considered while ensuring patients' security on hospital premises.

(129) (C) She should have immediately evacuated the infants with their oxygen supplies to a safe room.

The immediate evacuation of critically ill patients should be the priority in such situations. This is because all the other actions involve a time delay that could threaten patients' lives.

(130) (A) To connect a human to a machine.

An interface is when two things meet or connect. A human-machine interface connects a human to a machine or vice versa.

(131) (C) Equitable distribution of health-care resources among the patients.

An equal distribution of health-care facilities ensures better patient safety. The number of patients, the popularity of the hospital and the paramedical staff's experience have no bearing on improving patient safety.

(132) (D) Patient safety.

To check if quality standards are being met in a health-care organization, patient safety programs are a key metric.

(133) (A) Failures are identified and reduced on a regular basis.

An exceptionally reliable health-care organization is one that prioritizes patient safety and identifies failures in the system.

(134)   (A) The foundation for improving the quality of health care across the organization.

A quality framework is responsible for establishing the improvement of quality in a health-care organization.

(135)   (B) Neonatal intensive care unit.

The NICU is a designated unit in a hospital where intensive care is provided to critically ill newborn babies.

(136)   (C) They tell you the location of the baby in real time.

Real-time protection mechanisms allow you to locate babies and their kidnappers easily.

(137)   (A) Human factor engineering.

Human factor engineering ensures maximum safety and reduces errors in a system by taking into consideration the fact that people are fallible.

(138)   (A) Patient safety programs.

Patient safety programs ensure the provision of maximum security and better health-care facilities to patients by analyzing and assessing errors.

(139)   (B) Assessing patient-centric risks.

Risk management plans and assessments are carried out to identify patient safety errors; thus, assessing patient-centric risks should be the ultimate priority for these plans and assessments.

(140)   (A) Lead from the front.

The leader or the head of a particular department or organization should always lead from the front to instill confidence among subordinates. This also enables the immediate correction of any errors in procedures being carried out.

Made in the USA
Columbia, SC
17 April 2023